374·1   £19.99   Ⓐ

+ CD in back
of book

 **OW TO MANAGE BEHAVIOUR IN FURTHER
EDUCATION**

HOW TO MANAGE BEHAVIOUR IN FURTHER EDUCATION

Dave Vizard

P·C·P

Paul Chapman
Publishing

First published 2007

Paul Chapman Publishing
A SAGE Publications Company
1 Oliver's Yard
55 City Road
London EC1Y 1SP

SAGE Publications Inc
2455 Teller Road
Thousand Oaks, California 91320

SAGE Publications India Pvt Ltd
B1/I 1 Mohan Cooperative Industrial Area
Mathura Road, Post Bag 7
New Delhi 110 044

Library of Congress Control Number: 2007921905

A catalogue record for this book is available from the British Library

ISBN 978-1-4129-3455-8
ISBN 978-1-4129-3456-5 (pbk)

Typeset by Pantek Arts Ltd, Maidstone, Kent
Printed in Great Britain by Cromwell Press Ltd, Trowbridge, Wiltshire
Printed on paper from sustainable resources

CONTENTS

CONTENTS OF THE CD ROM

The accompanying CD Rom contains 20 tried and tested staff development activities used by the author in Further Education Colleges throughout the UK. The resources on the CD are downloadable and amendable. Throughout the book you will also see this icon used, which tells you that there is an electronic version of the material available on the CD Rom.

From Chapter 3

Reflection on Practice: Weekly Behaviour Management Log

From Chapter 4
Reflection on Practice:
      Physical Environment Questionnaire
      Peripheral Learning Questionnaire
      Positive Behaviour Management Questionnaire

From Chapter 9
Reflection on Practice: Strategies for facing challenging behaviour

From Chapter 11
Staff Development Activities
      Activity 1:   Our Top Ten
      Activity 2:   Audits for Staff
      Activity 3:   Positive Learning Environment – 10 Rs
      Activity 4:   Endorphin Release
      Activity 5:   See and Hear
      Activity 6:   Blocking and 'Broken Record' Technique
      Activity 7:   Role Play
      Activity 8:   True Lies!
      Activity 9:   The 4 Fs of Confrontation
      Activity 10:   Communication Blockers
      Activity 11:   Active Listening
      Activity 12:   Language of Choice
      Activity 13:   How Your College Helps Students to Develop Their Own Strategies to Manage Their Behaviour
      Activity 14:   Wheels Within Wheels
      Activity 15:   Hot Seating
      Activity 16:   Identifying Key Student Roles in Badly Behaving Groups
      Activity 17:   Picture This
      Activity 18:   Assertiveness 'Thought Shower'
      Activity 19:   Being Assertive with Students
      Activity 20:   What Do You Do Next?
                         Case Studies A–M

ABOUT THE AUTHOR

Dave Vizard is an independent consultant who regularly trains lecturers, teachers and support workers around the country on behaviour management. His years of experience in the field translate into realistic, and frequently entertaining, advice.

Dave lectures at Plymouth University on the Foundation Degree, and trains extensively throughout the UK in colleges of FE. He has 35 years of experience in education in a variety of settings. He has also trained trainers for the Learning and Skills Network (formerly Learning and Skills Development Agency) in Behaviour Management. Dave has set up his own consultancy company, Behaviour Solutions, who provide INSET training for schools and colleges of FE.

For more information about other publications by the author, a free newsletter and information about quality staff development provided by Behaviour Solutions, visit Dave's website: **www.behavioursolutions.com**.

Acknowledgements

Many thanks to my son, Tim Vizard, for all his hard work in typing and copy reading this book. Thanks to my wife, Annwyn, daughter, Emma and my Mum, without whose support this book would not have been possible. Special thanks should also be extended to all the staff in the Further Education Colleges with whom I have worked over many years.

HOW TO USE THIS BOOK

This book contains practical strategies for successfully managing the behaviour of learners in Further Education Colleges. It focuses on 14–16 year olds learners but the strategies are equally appropriate for older learners. Each chapter has a synopsis of content at the beginning and a summary of key points at the end, which are particularly useful for busy people. Each chapter has a section where you can reflect on your own practice. There are also examples of good practice from colleges.

The accompanying CD Rom contains 20 tried and tested staff development activities used by the author in Further Education Colleges throughout the UK. The resources on the CD are downloadable and amendable. Throughout the book you will also see this icon used, which tells you that there is an electronic version of the material available on the CD Rom.

Why are some 14–16 year olds in Further Education?

This chapter looks at:

■ how policy and provision in the sector has developed

■ the benefits for 14–16 year old learners of being in Further Education (FE)

■ key issues with younger learners in FE – for example, Health and Safety, Duty of Care

■ the challenges 14–16 year olds pose compared with 16–19 year olds

■ developing an understanding of 14–16 year olds' behaviour:

❏ causes of behaviour problems and being a 14–16 year old

❏ brain re-configuration in adolescents and its effect on learning and behaviour

❏ understanding and supporting special and additional needs – Attention Deficit Hyperactivity Disorder (ADHD), Asperger Syndrome, Oppositional Defiant Disorder (ODD), Tourette Syndrome and Conduct Disorder (CD)

❏ key characteristics and useful techniques and strategies

How policy and provision has developed in the sector relating to 14–16 year olds

Many students in the past have become severely disaffected with their school experience and a curriculum that did not meet their needs. As a result, truancy levels rose as did the rates of exclusion, as many students were lost from the education system. Policy makers felt there was a need to re-engage these learners and get young people to stay in education longer. Developing a wide range of learning experiences and greater coherence for students in the 14–19 range was seen as critical.

Our aim at 14–19 is to transform the learning experience for young people, so that by the age of 16 they are committed to continued learning, whether in school, college or the workplace. And we want to help every young person to fulfil their potential. (DfES, 2003)

Increased Flexibility Programme

In 2002 the Increased Flexibility Programme (IFP) was developed to create enhanced vocational and work-related learning opportunities for 14–16 year olds in Further Education. This enabled school students to work in college for a period of time each week or for longer periods in the case of excluded students. This had the effect of re-engaging large numbers of students and was very successful in increasing post-16 participation.

14–19 Education and Skills White Paper (DfES, 2005)

As part of this White Paper the idea of partnership working was introduced, with improved links between schools and colleges being essential. The idea was to develop areas of specialisation reflecting the needs of local areas. The White Paper stated that 14–19 year olds should be able to study courses in the institution best placed to meet their needs and interests. The paper stated that it wanted to increase post-16 participation from 75 per cent to 90 per cent by 2015. New Specialized Diplomas were to be introduced and would be a national entitlement for all 14–19 year olds by 2013. In addition, 14–16 year olds would be able to continue core and foundation subject study and also be able to choose to take the new employer-led Specialized Diploma. Fourteen lines of learning were to be linked to broader skills in the Specialized Diplomas. Also generic learning was developed in relation to Functional Skills (functional skills in English, Maths and ICT) and a Skills Framework (Personal, Learning and Thinking Skills).

The introduction of a statutory requirement for Careers Education and Guidance (CEG) has led to a national framework for quality guidance. CEG is now part of the Ofsted Inspection Process. Also, the introduction of Individual Learning Plans (ILPs) will get students to plan at the end of Key Stage 3 (14 years of age) their education and training across the whole of the 14–19 range. With enhanced CEG and ILPs, students will be making more informed choices for their post-14 education.

The benefits for 14–16 year olds of being in FE

For some learners their experience of school is negative. They are frequently in trouble and receive a large number of sanctions. They feel that they are being picked on – 'damned if we do, damned if we don't'. Many learners have found it difficult to engage with an education system based on content-led courses that involve lots of reading and writing. Their literacy skills are limited and much of the reading material is five to six years ahead of their reading age. They attempt to avoid the challenge of the page. Many have found notoriety by 'being good at being bad'. Many of the students I have interviewed who present behavioural problems in schools are kinaesthetic learners – and schools expect them to sit still for long periods of time. So learners love the practical experiences they get in FE colleges – they can experience success for once in their lives. The things they find more beneficial are:

- practical subjects give them a kinaesthetic outlet

- they can work in an adult environment

- the environment is very positive and first names are used

- courses have a greater relationship with the world of work – allows them to test potential career pathways

- the better range of courses has more relevance

- courses are better suited to their skills

Reflection on practice

What are the benefits for a Further Education College of having 14–16 year old learners on site?

1. _____

   _____

2. _____

   _____

3. _____

   _____

4. _____

   _____

5. _____

   _____

The challenges posed by 14–16 year olds compared with 16–19 year olds

The way behaviour is managed and the ethos of schools may be quite different from colleges and this can cause challenging behaviour from learners whilst they acclimatize to the different approaches found in colleges. A few of the difficulties learners face which can lead to challenging behaviour are:

- lack of maturity

- inability to handle the increased freedom from unsupervised time

- unable to cope with the large size of the college

- difficulty in managing their time

- fear of being split up from peer group

- frightened of challenge and being taken out of their comfort zone

- difficulty in adapting to Health and Safety requirements

Key issues relating to young learners – Health and Safety, Duty of Care

Duty of Care

Working with 14–16 year old learners raises issues relating to Duty of Care. If the student is on the school roll and is at the college part-time then the responsibility rests with the student's school. It is important to ensure school partners and parents/carers understand where responsibility for Duty of Care lies. The following points need to be made clear to parents/carers:

- students are not supervised at lunchtime

- there may be other times of the day when they are unsupervised

- they will come into contact with older teenagers and adults on the college site

- unless school makes different arrangements, students will travel from and to school independently

- the college is an open-access location

Risk Assessment

All activities that 14–16 year olds are likely to carry out need to be risk assessed and appropriate insurances must be gained. Further issues relating to Health and Safety will be dealt with in Chapter 2.

Developing an understanding of 14–16 year olds' behaviour

Some students spend their lives creating conflict waiting for the reaction from those around them. If there is no reaction, their behaviour becomes progressively worse until there is a reaction.

Causes of behaviour problems and being a 14–16 year old today

- Many learners have incredibly low self-esteem because of the many negative experiences they have had

- 'Factory farming' – testing from the age of 5 has led to some learners wishing to dis-engage from the learning process and displaying challenging behaviour as a way of gaining recognition

- Students are getting conflicting and mixed messages of what is expected of them – all learners need a consistent voice

- Society has stated the importance of children's rights. In some ways this has developed an 'inverted society' where adults are expected to fit around the needs of children

■ Many students are under immense pressure from their peer group. Anti-social behaviour for some groups is seen as 'a badge of honour'. For example, drinking, abusive and threatening behaviour or damaging, graffitying property. This can be further extended to drug taking and promiscuous/sexual activity. Many students feel pressurized – join in or become a victim

■ These pressures can lead to mental health issues – eating disorders, self-harm, suicide. Many learners have experienced such bad experiences through separation, violence and media images that they are suffering from Post-Traumatic Stress Disorder (PTSD)

■ Home background

❑ Many parents do not have the necessary parenting skills – they are looking for someone to 'save' their child

❑ Some parents will challenge every action by school/college – the 'all rights, no responsibility' parents

❑ Breakdown of the family unit

❑ Breakdown of the extended family – footloose nature of families with supporting family members far away

❑ Little time for support from family members and some members live far away

❑ Family meal time is a thing of the past – a nation of grazers, eating finger-friendly products, is on the rise

❑ Aggressive role models in the home

❑ No restrictions/control – children wander around the community without restraint

■ Television/Media/Internet

❑ Students come to college disrupted because of the images they see on television from news bulletins and the violent themes in 'soaps'. These images are particularly telling as young people become addicted to soaps. Some of the topics on radio can also be quite disturbing, as can the lyrics to songs

❑ Easy access to films on DVD can lead to students seeing disturbing and aggressive content

❑ Some video games are quite violent and can have a desensitizing effect causing people to become unnaturally violent when faced with challenge

❑ Easy access to very disturbing images on the Internet can be distressing

■ Food for thought

❑ Students do not re-hydrate sufficiently. We should drink approximately 1.2 litres of water a day (Food Standards Agency, 2006); instead students consume coffee, colas and other drinks that have a diuretic effect. As the brain is made up of more than 80 per cent water (Blakemore and Frith, 2005:18) and uses 30 per cent of all water consumed (Vizard, 2004a: 6), dehydration can have a severe impact on behaviour and the ability to learn

❑ Many of the fast foods and ready prepared food items that are consumed, are full of additives, which can severely affect behaviour

❑ Increasing intake of fish oil supplements can improve behaviour and learning in students (see further Blakemore and Frith, 2005: 186)

❑ Increasing zinc and iron intake has also been shown to improve behaviour (see further Northern, 2004).

Brain reconfiguration in adolescence and its effect on learning and behaviour

Prior to birth and throughout life pruning of brain cells takes place. Giedd (2004, cited in Wallis, 2004) suggested that at the age of 11 in girls and $12\frac{1}{2}$ years in boys, a key phase of pruning takes place, continuing up until around the age of 25. During this time the adolescent pre-frontal cortex is smaller than in younger children. Some brain areas shrink back to allow others maximum resources whilst they develop. Because of the pruning and change in configuration, adolescents:

- are very impulsive

- love risk taking because this generates rushes of the hormone dopamine

- cannot easily assess causes and effects of their actions

- are less able to assess threats

- are ruled by emotions more than logic

- are unable easily to recover from trauma

The area of the brain that reconfigures first is the part that controls sensory preference – the visual, auditory, kinaesthetic, olfactory and gustatory. As the brain reconfigures the more rational regions of the upper cortex we see the following:

- development of attributes associated with maturity

- calmer outlook

- stable moods

- decrease in risk taking

- ability to reason and think things through

When the pre-frontal cortex is reconfigured students are able to:

- plan

- set priorities

- organize thoughts

- suppress impulses

- weigh up consequences of their actions

There is a later maturation of the frontal lobes in Western society because of the longer period of dependency upon parents and the associated abdication of adult responsibilities. Many are 'helicopter parents', hovering over the children, doing everything for them. Young people are now staying at home longer because of living costs, scarcity of jobs and, due to increases in tuition fees, many attend local Higher Education Institutions to save on accommodation costs. However, we see an early maturation of the frontal lobes in young adults in other societies due to their having to assume responsibilities at a much earlier age.

Reflection on practice

Using the information on brain reconfiguration in adolescence, list five ways in which you could use this information to adapt your teaching, learning and behaviour management strategies with 14–16 year old learners.

1. _____

_____

2. _____

_____

3. _____

_____

4. _____

_____

5. _____

_____

Understanding and Supporting Special and Additional Needs

A number of learners will suffer from several conditions and syndromes. For example:

- 50–65 per cent of children diagnosed with Oppositional Defiant Disorder (ODD) have Attention Deficit Hyperactivity Disorder (ADHD) (Kuhne et al., 1997, cited in Chandler, 2006)

- 30–50 per cent of children diagnosed with Conduct Disorder (CD) have ADHD (Kuhne et al., 1997, cited in Chandler, 2006)

- 50 per cent of children with Tourette Syndrome have ADHD (Diprose and Burge, 2003)

It is not unusual for some young people to have three or four conditions, such as CD, Tourette Syndrome, ADHD and Obsessive Compulsive Disorder (OCD). These conditions are discussed over the following pages, based on my own experiences and published work (Vizard, 2006), work with Teaching Assistants (TAs) at Plymouth University and other research cited below.

Autism

Characteristics Autistic students spend their time engaged in puzzling and disturbing behaviours. Three areas have been identified:

- impairment in social interaction

- impairment in communication

- restricted and repetitive patterns of behaviour

Diprose and Burge (2003) listed the following characteristics:

- difficulty in relating to people, events or even objects – isolation preferred

- delays in language and cognitive development – limited intellectual ability

- impaired social interaction

- unconventional use of toys

- avoidance of eye contact

- insistence on routine and environment remaining unchanged

- repetitive movements – rocking, spinning, head banging

- unusual sleep patterns – can stay up all night

Treatment/strategies

- **Developing communication/language** – helping students to learn ways to communicate, initially by using sign language and pictures rather than verbal language. Using visual cues/cards is important. Using speech and drama to help with conversation, not keeping thoughts to themselves – encourage thinking, teaching them opening comments for conversations, getting them to ask for help

- **Social skills** – teaching them to play and share, helping them with their emotional literacy, using cooperative learning, helping them to understand and express their emotions. Reassure and praise

- **Behaviour management** – environment should be structured and predictable. Unstructured time is when problems can arise – so structure to the day is needed, also time out strategies are useful. When poor behaviour displayed refer to rules and insist they are kept. Remain calm and keep volume down

- **Motor coordination** – to help with clumsiness, exercises and games may need to be developed. Writing can be supported through keyboards

Further reading:

> www.autism.org
>
> www.nas.org
>
> www.wikipedia/org/wiki/Autism
>
> www.paains/org.uk

Asperger Syndrome (AS)

Characteristics Students with AS often have the following characteristics:

- ■ **Difficulty with social relationships**

  - ❏ Want to be sociable and enjoy human contact

  - ❏ Find difficulty in understanding how others feel

  - ❏ Find it hard to read non-verbal communication including facial expression

  - ❏ Find it hard to maintain eye contact

- ■ **Difficulty with communication**

  - ❏ It is difficult for them to have a two-way conversation, taking all the time to speak without wanting to listen. They do not check the reaction of listeners

  - ❏ They have difficulty communicating feelings and reactions to others

  - ❏ When faced with challenge they may run away and hide or vent their frustration through temper or tantrum

  - ❏ They can be over-precise and over-literal. Turns of phrase and metaphors can cause alarm. Jokes and exaggerated language can also cause a problem

- ■ **Emotionally fragile**

  - ❏ They can be self-critical and easily become stressed. Some students have difficulties coping with everyday life. Changes in routines and transitions can be difficult

- ■ **Special interests**

  - ❏ People with AS can develop an almost obsessive interest in a hobby or interest in arranging or memorising facts about a special subject such as train timetables or football results

- ■ **Verbal IQ is lower than performance IQ**

Treatment/strategies

- ■ There is no specific treatment. It is possible for a student with AS to acquire social skills

■ The demands of adolescence mean a student with AS is likely to be under considerable stress at that time. Teach them relaxation techniques to be calm – breathing exercises, stress balls

■ Establish a clear achievable routine – use posters to provide visual information

■ Provide a structured, consistent and predictable environment

■ Give positive feedback whenever possible

Attention Deficit Hyperactivity Disorder (ADHD)

Characteristics Students with ADHD cannot block out the stimuli that constantly surround us (noise, smells and texture). They are continually distracted by them and therefore find it difficult to focus on one task only

ADHD manifests itself in three main ways:

■ Hyperactivity

■ Impulsiveness

■ Inattention

Treatment/strategies

■ Create a structured, predictable environment. Consistent seating arrangements, rules, expectations and logical consequences (consequences of behaviour have to be instant) (Jensen, 2005)

■ Give clear, precise instructions starting with student's name and ensuring eye contact. Repeat, using 'broken record' technique if necessary

■ Position them in class where they are least likely to be distracted (sit away from known distractions)

■ Try to keep noise level low and prevent distractions

■ Use dramatherapy and creative arts

■ Use of headphones

■ Dietary adaptation – omega fatty acids

■ Break up tasks into attainable steps

Further reading:

O'Regan, F. (2002) *How to Teach and Manage Children with ADHD*. Wisbech: LDA

www.ADDERS.org – run by a parent with a child with ADHD

www.CHADD.org – USA ADHD support group

Oppositional Defiant Disorder (ODD)

Characteristics Students with ODD often have the following characteristics:

- Frequent temper tantrums
- Excessive arguing with adults
- Active defiance and refusal to comply with adult requests and rules
- Often deliberately annoy people
- Spiteful and vindictive
- Seek revenge

Treatment/strategies

- Develop a Behaviour Plan – when doing this we must remember that the basic drive of a student with ODD is to resist the control and manipulation from any adult. The more controlling the adult appears to be, the more oppositional the student becomes
- These students need structure, rules, rewards, guidance and a sense of safety. They need a structured environment which reminds them frequently of acceptable behaviour limits and expectations
- Behaviour modification techniques including anger management should be used
- Rewards need to be tangible and they need to be rewarded immediately following the correct behaviour

Conduct Disorder (CD)

Characteristics A repetitive and persistent pattern of behaviour in which the basic rights of others are violated. The following characteristics are based on the *Diagnostic and Statistical Manual of the American Psychiatric Association* (cited in O'Regan, 2002):

- Aggression
  - ❏ bullies, threatens or intimidates others
  - ❏ initiates fights
  - ❏ uses weapons that could harm others
  - ❏ steals from a victim whilst confronting them
- Destruction of property
- Deceitfulness, lying or stealing
- Serious violation of rules

Treatment/strategies:

■ Need structure – rules, rewards, guidance and a sense of included safety.

Further reading:

www.aacap.org – American Academy of Child and Adolescent Psychiatry

Tourette Syndrome

Characteristics Symptoms of Tourette Syndrome can be divided into:

■ Motor – it is a neurological disorder characterized by tics which are involuntary, rapid and sudden movements that occur repeatedly in the same way

■ Vocal – involuntary noises or vocalizations

■ Behavioural – self-destructive behaviours may occur

Treatment/strategies

■ Most people with Tourette Syndrome do not require medication. Medication can help in severe cases and can suppress tics and make life more manageable. These drugs increase the amount of dophamine in the body but can have side effects

■ Behaviour therapies and techniques: for example, encouraging students to practise a common tic may allow them to have a tic-free episode afterwards (as people with Tourette Syndrome have to make a certain number of tics each day)

■ Exercise and relaxation techniques help

■ Some students seem to be helped by removing additives from their diet. Herbal medicines, vitamin and mineral supplements can help

Further reading:

www.tourettes-disorder.com

Key points

■ Policy and provision in the sector relating to 14–16 year olds:

❑　　　Impact of Increased Flexibility Programme in re-engaging large numbers of students increasing post-16 participation

❑　　　Increase in partnership working through 14–19 Education and Skills White Paper

❑　　　Increase in post-16 participation to 90 per cent by 2015

❑　　　Introduction of Specialized Diplomas, Functional Skills and Skills Framework

❑　　　Statutory 11–19 Careers Education and Guidance

❑　　　Individual Learning Plans (end KS3)

- ■ Benefits of being in FE for 14–16 year old learners

  - ❏ Experience courses of greater relevance to them

  - ❏ Practical subjects to utilize kinaesthetic energy

  - ❏ Working in an adult, positive environment

- ■ Challenges they pose

  - ❏ Many learners will take a short period to acclimatize, aided by appropriate induction programme

- ■ Key issues relating to Health and Safety, Duty of Care

  - ❏ Working with pre-16 learners in compulsory education you need to establish with school and parents/carers the boundaries of your Duty of Care

- ■ Developing an understanding of 14–16 year old behaviours

  - ❏ Many learners have low self-esteem

  - ❏ 'Factory farming' techniques with learners mean many have tasted failure

  - ❏ Immense pressure from peer group

  - ❏ Variety of mental health issues

  - ❏ Home background

  - ❏ Effects of media

  - ❏ Effects of food

- ■ Brain re-configuration in adolescence and its effect on learning and behaviour. There are many changes to the brain in adolescence leading to learners being:

  - ❏ Impulsive

  - ❏ Risk taking

  - ❏ Unable to assess causes and effects

  - ❏ Less able to assess threats

  - ❏ Ruled by emotions

  - ❏ Unable easily to recover from trauma

Only when the pre-frontal cortex is fully developed are learners able to plan, set priorities, organize thoughts, suppress impulses and weigh up consequences of their actions

- ■ Understanding and supporting special and additional needs

  - ❏ Individual students can suffer from a number of conditions, for example, 50 per cent of children with Tourette Syndrome have ADHD

  - ❏ The following conditions: Autism, Asperger Syndrome, ADHD, ODD, CD and Tourette Syndrome, are listed with key symptoms/characteristics and strategies to use with them

CHAPTER 2

Establishing and developing effective links with partner schools

This chapter looks at:

■ ways to develop collaborative working

■ ways to develop effective induction and team building

■ getting to grips with gritty issues of logistics and planning

■ mutual understanding of each sector:

❑ interpreting Key Stage 3 (KS3) data

❑ making best use of Individual Education Plans (IEP)

■ developing good communication channels

■ ensuring students with Special Educational Needs (SEN) have appropriate support

■ joint understanding of key Health and Safety issues

■ developing a longer-term planning cycle, to ensure necessary resources are available – such as staff and facilities

Ways to develop collaborative working

Changes in the delivery of the 14–19 curriculum are resulting in more collaborative working between schools and colleges – for example, clusters of schools are developing partnerships with colleges to deliver Specialized Diplomas. However, when the Increased Flexibility Programme (IFP) was first introduced the links between schools and colleges were not as effective as they might have been in some areas. Some lecturers felt that the schools only put the most poorly behaved students on the programme. Also many lecturers were of the view that they had entered lecturing to teach post-compulsory school age students and were not trained to teach students below 16 years of age. Some students were also allocated places on courses that were inappropriate.

Following these initial teething problems, the IFP has been a great success. Excellent links have been established and developed between partner schools and colleges. Where links have worked well this has been owing to:

- time being allocated for joint planning and preparation

- a Planning Cycle allowing for planning well in advance, with appropriate resourcing

- school staff and lecturers involved in joint staff development activities

- lecturers being given appropriate support and staff development on behaviour management relating to 14–16 year olds

- lecturers being given support to interpret school data relating to students' ability and therefore successfully pitching the work at an appropriate level

- coordinating staff clearly identified in each sector so that communication is easier

- good information exchange systems in place

- students well informed about the course content

- clear guidance given to students on what is expected of them in College and the differences in ethos in a post-compulsory setting

- an agreed behaviour management policy relating to college, made between schools and colleges in the partnership

Ways to develop effective induction and team building

Below are some important points relating to effective induction and team building.

- College and school staff involved with 14–16 year old learners should meet to make the necessary preparation for each cohort

- Teams of lecturers involved in working with 14–16 year olds should meet for necessary planning prior to induction of each cohort – given the challenge of staffing, rising numbers of younger learners and the part-time nature of staffing this can be difficult to achieve

- It is also important that students are allocated places on appropriate courses. For this to occur:

  ❏ students need to understand what each course involves

  ❏ some students do not understand the requirements of practical subjects and therefore find it difficult to adapt to the course. To overcome this Taster Days, where students can sample what a number of courses have to offer, have been useful. Also, college students have returned to their former schools to explain from a student's perspective what each course is likely to involve. I have seen these students bringing in clothing, safety gear and the equipment/tools they need to use on their course

❑ enough places need to be available on each course to meet student demand. In reality this is difficult to achieve as there is a finite amount of workshop/practical area space. Also, rapidly expanding numbers of students have led to difficulties in staff recruitment

❑ students interviews have stated that not getting on their first choice course has led to bitter disappointment. Some lecturers report that this has led to resentment and challenging behaviour

■ There should be a clear application and interview process where students apply to courses and are interviewed by college staff, including in some cases senior college staff

■ Issue booklets that clearly outline expectations of college, including code of conduct and rules

■ Get school staff and college lecturers to outline the differences between school and college with students prior to the start of the course

■ Have team building sessions in term prior to students starting the course. It is important to get students from different schools together. Information on group bonding sessions will be given in Chapter 3

Getting to grips with the gritty issues of logistics and planning

When groups of students come from a variety of schools, each with their varying timings of school day, different codes of behaviour, different expectations and different reporting systems, it can be a real challenge to coordinate these systems and to develop a meaningful experience for learners.

Some key areas to consider are given below:

■ Timetable congruence

❑ Some colleges have variable start times for groups of students from different schools. However, this can provide a real challenge for lecturers of practical subjects

❑ Where it works best, schools and college, through compromise, agree a common start time

■ Transport

❑ To get all students into college can be a problem, particularly when coaches/buses are usually fully used for transporting school students at the beginning of the day and so may not be available until later

❑ One approach could be to delay the start of the day slightly, so that transport is available

❑ Transport back to school can affect students' ability to engage in fuller aspects of college life

❑ Health and Safety and Duty of Care issues can affect students making their own way to college

■ Uniform

❑ To wear uniform or not to wear uniform is a key issue. Wearing school uniform can be a problem for students as it does not permit full integration and makes them feel different. Some schools can insist students wear uniform as it is easier to identify them. The best solution is for students to dress casually or wear uniforms associated with the areas they are working in, such as hospitality and catering (e.g. chefs'/waiters' clothing) or hair and beauty

■ Reporting

❑ Schools use different reporting systems. It works best where a common reporting system is used by the college which can feed information back to the school on the progress of learners

❑ Colleges also need minimum key data on students relating to ability, attendance and behavioural issues. When there are behavioural problems, a school contact is needed to relay key information back to the school

■ Support for learners with SEN

❑ An agreement needs to be made between colleges and individual schools on the level of support allocated to individual learners. It is essential that support workers come with learners and support them in college

■ Behaviour management

❑ A clear policy on behaviour management is needed, so that all schools and students agree to the mutually agreed policy

Mutual understanding of each sector

One issue that can cause a communication problem between the sectors is the widespread use of specialist terms and acronyms. To help you, a Glossary has been included at the end of the book (see p.153).

Reflection on practice

List any terms/acronyms from the school sector that have arisen in your practice that you do not understand and for which you need to seek an explanation/definition (see page 153 for websites with full definitions).

1. _____

    _____

2. _____

    _____

3. _____

    _____

4. _____

    _____

5. _____

    _____

Interpreting Key Stage 3 data

Schools hold a large quantity of data on students. It is useful for colleges to have key elements of this data to help them understand the ability of individual students, their learning and behaviour profiles.

Baseline Assessments are given when students arrive at secondary school at the age of 11. Often a Cognitive Ability Test (CAT) is given, which gives a score from standardized tests in verbal, non-verbal reasoning and mathematical skills. It gives an indication of a student's potential and this data together with end of Key Stage 2 (taken at 11 years of age) assessments is used to predict the likely level that the student will achieve at the end of Key Stage 3 (taken at 14 years of age). This data can be used for target setting and for calculating the value-added by the school during a student's career. The National Curriculum Assessments' Standard Assessment Test (SATs) are held at the end of each of the Key Stages. The National Curriculum Assessments test a number of Attainment Targets (AT) for each subject. A target sets out the knowledge, skills and understanding, students are expected to reach. There are 8 levels for each AT and the Attainment Level (AL) is the level at which a student is working. At Key Stage 3 (KS3) the great majority of students are expected to work within the range of Levels 3–7. The expected attainment for the majority of students at the end of KS3 is Levels 5–6.

Teacher assessments are used in conjunction with SATs. Sometimes additional assessments are used, such as the Middle Years Information Systems (Mid YIS). These test ability and aptitude for learning. Tests comprise of vocabulary, mathematics and non-verbal reasoning. Additional tests assess writing speed, listening and comprehension skills. Graphs are produced which give level predictions for end of KS3 and place students in one of four bands, A–D, with A the highest and D the lowest. Additional information is held on attendance and there will be a behaviour log for each student. Key information on students with Special Educational Needs will also be held. More details on this will be given later in the chapter.

Making best use of Individual Learning Plans

Individual Learning Plans completed by students towards the end of Key Stage 3 at 14 years of age are essential with the increasing flexibility at Key Stage 4 and the variety of progression routes from 16 years of age. They plan the education and training across the 14–19 range. They list progress and achievement at 14, including SATs results at KS2 and 3, and choices of subject and target grades for KS4. They highlight ideas for Work Experience and outline the broad learning and career goals for the 14–19 phase. They can be developed by being linked to recording in the Progress File – a set of materials designed to support the processes of planning, reaching goals and receiving progress. The Progress File replaces the Record of Achievement (ROA). I have been associated with the Progress File from its initial development – being involved in one of the pilot schemes. It provides a basis for monitoring and review of progress throughout the 14–19 phase. ILPs can link in with the Personal Learning and Thinking Skills (PLTS) of the 14–19 curriculum.

Reflection on practice

What are the key pieces of information/data from schools that you need on 14–16 year old learners to ensure that you can manage their behaviour and get the best work from them initially?

1. _____

_____

2. _____

_____

3. _____

_____

4. _____

_____

5. _____

_____

Developing good communication channels

Where IFP schemes have worked well there has been excellent communication between colleges and schools. Schools have provided colleges with key information on students prior to the commencement of the programme. Once the programme is under way the college feeds schools with key information on the progress of individual students outlining performance, achievement and progress. Should there be any behaviour problems this information is relayed. If students know that there is effective communication they are less likely to display challenging behaviour.

Ensuring students with SEN have appropriate support

School students with behavioural or learning difficulties are assessed and those at School Action or School Action Plus level are likely to have an Individual Education Plan written, which outlines a student's special educational needs and explains how the school is making arrangements to meet these. Some students will be given additional support from a teaching assistant (TA). These will be allocated on a part- or full-time basis. Students with extreme learning difficulties – such as those whose performance levels do not reach National Curriculum Level 1 – are placed on P scales. The P levels are P1–3 across all subjects. When transferring to college many students with SEN are lost in the system because schools have not informed the college of their IEPs or needs.

Also the TA support allocated to the student does not always transfer to the college with the student. Individual TAs may be allocated to a number of students in school and when they come to college they are faced with the possible dilemma that their students may be in several areas. Some colleges have re-allocated TAs to subject areas where they will support several students, sometimes not those from their own school. Permission has to be sought for this to occur and training may be necessary, but this reduces the problem of TAs being expected to be in two places at once. It is important for lecturers to be aware of the special educational needs of students and support strategies that are effective.

Joint understanding of key Health and Safety issues

With 14–16 year olds being of compulsory school age there are key issues concerned with Duty of Care and Health and Safety that need addressing. These issues include:

- What supervision is needed during lunch breaks and other free time during the day?
- Who is responsible for students on the way to and from college?
- What are the Health and Safety issues relating to practical/workshop areas, relating to use of equipment, tools etc.?
- Who provides Health and Safety training for students?
- Who conducts Health and Safety checks?
- Due to the broad age range of students in college – are there issues relating to safety of younger students?

Health and Safety issues need to be fully discussed and agreed by all partners.

Developing a longer-term planning cycle to ensure resources are available

The short-term nature of funding and variation in staffing levels led to difficulties in longer-term planning initially. Also, the rapidly expanding nature of the 14–16 programme led to great difficulties in projecting student numbers. Employing part-time staff for these learners was also challenging because of skill shortages and only short-term contracts being available. With developments in the 14–19 curriculum, including Specialized Diplomas, it will now be possible to plan to ensure staffing and facilities are available.

Key points to remember

- Ensure there is full development of collaborative working in partnerships to deliver Specialized Diplomas

- Ensure appropriate resources are made available for joint planning, staff development and information exchange

- Spend time ensuring that appropriate induction and team building activities are in place

- Try to overcome the challenges relating to lack of timetable congruence and transport

- Ensure that there is appropriate information exchange

- Support for learners with SEN is essential; lecturers need to know about students with IEPs

- Help lecturers to understand and interpret key school data

- Ensure that there are appropriate communication channels – with a named contact in each institution

- Addressing Health and Safety and Duty of Care issues with 14–16 year old learners is essential

CHAPTER 3

Making a strong first impression

This chapter looks at:

■ bringing together groups from different schools – appropriate induction and group bonding strategies

■ making a significant initial impact on students and getting initial interactions right

■ the importance of establishing rules, routines and protocols

■ key skills and strategies needed to be successful with 14–16 year old learners

Bringing together groups from different schools

In Chapter 2 we discussed some key elements of developing effective induction from the viewpoint of interviewing and appropriate course selection. However, one important area that also needs to be considered is how to bring together groups of students from different schools and to bond them as a group. Bringing together very strong alpha males and alpha females (refer to Chapter 8) from different schools will lead to friction as they battle for supremacy. A lot of disruptive and challenging behaviour will occur until they can gain a clear pecking order.

In many schemes students from different schools are brought together prior to the commencement of the course. A carefully constructed series of group bonding activities then occur. Some examples are listed below:

■ Trust exercises

  ❏ Guiding partner around room/college site whilst they are blindfolded

  ❏ Guiding partner to stick labels on a poster

■ 'Now Get Out Of That' challenges

  ❏ In teams, moving a piece of equipment over obstacles or imaginary ravines

■ Getting groups to develop map outlines out of rope

■ Setting up a campsite using six tents – in appropriate locations

The aim of setting up such activities is to develop cooperation and socialization amongst group members. It will develop positivity and cohesion. If the activities involve a high level of challenge then it will help with group bonding. Each group would be given a list of areas that their group would be assessed upon during the activity. For example:

■ total group involvement

■ constructive communication

■ positive cooperation

■ good discipline and behaviour

■ sensible use of personal skills within groups

■ attention to Health and Safety

Making a significant initial impact on students

Students know teachers have buttons to push and they will push them. (Wragg, 2002)

The impact that you make during the first few minutes when you meet a group is critical. Imagine each student as a mini bar-code scanner: as they arrive they will zap you, reading your body language and vocal tone. They will assess your hot buttons, what triggers you and makes you angry, what they are likely to get away with. They will throw down challenges to test you. Often these will occur from several students at once to see how effectively you manage multiple events. Students are very effective at 'testing the water'. They are also likely to have discussed with other students your reputation and will have built a useful profile.

It is important that you get your first interactions right. In behaviour management terms 14–16 year old learners will have been treated differently in schools, therefore, initially it may be necessary to be a person that you are not normally in the more adult setting of Further Education. Do not disclose too much verbally and keep your body language neutral. It is also important to mark your territory. Standing by the door to welcome students is important, it marks that they are leaving their social environment and entering your learning environment. It is essential that any initial challenges are dealt with effectively. Any weakness or vulnerability will be easily exposed. Giving the right presentation of self to students is key – be firm but friendly and avoid a pleading tone at all costs. Carefully rehearse your responses.

■ Be at the door to meet your group as they arrive. As they enter the room greet them and establish eye contact

■ Posture is important so stand in a confident manner with a straight back and head looking forward – a relaxed and confident bearing

■ When speaking to the students think about the tone of your voice and try to have command in your voice

■ When speaking to the whole group stand in a position where you can scan or 'lighthouse' the whole group. Position yourself in the classroom so that you have a wide field of vision. Try not to position yourself so that students are behind you. Scan the room repeatedly. Aim to make eye contact with as many students as possible. Some challenging and poorly behaved students will gravitate towards your 'blind spot' just in front of you

■ Use of silence can be very effective. Clint Eastwood used this to great effect in the 'Dollar' series of movies, and became 'a person of mystery'

■ Patrol the whole of the classroom and mark your territory. Remain mobile, move around mingling with the students – no-go areas should not exist

■ When students are working it is sometimes an effective strategy to stand at the back of the classroom, which can be a good controlling position

■ Ensure you allocate seats to the students and have a seating plan. Having named photographs is good as there is nothing more powerful than calling out a student's name when they are about to engage in some poor behaviour. Greet all students on entry to class and guide them to their allocated seats. For the first lesson it may be best to get students to line up outside. Remember you choose the seats, it is not an option for them to do this. Remember firm eye contact and a strong confident voice are necessary. If students choose to change places use the stop-watch to time the length of the disruption whilst they return to their normal places and detain them for the appropriate length of time

■ In the first few sessions make sure each transgression or example of poor behaviour is dealt with firmly

■ In the first few sessions try to anticipate when poor behaviour is likely to occur and intervene straight away. Dealing with incidents immediately stops them from escalating: 'The time to repair the roof is when the sun is shining.' (John F. Kennedy, State of the Union Address, 1 November 1962)

So it is essential that you are well organized and prepared, and create a firm yet confident image. The 'don't smile 'til Christmas' maxim may be useful, and it is certainly easier to loosen the reins than it is to tighten them, but even more powerful can be a relaxed, confident smile.

The importance of establishing rules, routines and protocols

■ Establish rules in the first session. Wait for quiet and then outline your rules for working. Clear boundaries need to be established and expectations regarding behaviour made clear. In practical areas there is a need to outline these in relation to key Health and Safety issues

■ Agree protocols for different types of work and for the beginning and ends of sessions. Establish a 'take-up time' at the beginning of each lesson – such as 2 minutes to settle. If students take longer, use the stop-watch to check duration of time wasting and detain them for this period. It is useful to have a take-up activity on the white board for students to do at the start

■ At the beginning of each session explain what work will be covered and the learning that will take place. This should be linked with the work covered in the previous session and show how it fits into the Big Picture

■ Agree how transitions will take place between different types of work

■ Make instructions clear and differentiate the work so all can achieve. Differentiation can be achieved through an understanding of an individual's needs based on test scores and target levels/grades

■ Have a strategy for settling the group at the end of the session and for the orderly exit of students. Issue of rewards earned during the session is a good strategy to use at the end. For exiting the room I run a Quiet Quiz. Standing at the front I ask questions quietly. The students at the front hear the question and answer them correctly and exit the room first. It is amazing how quickly the rest of the group become quiet. Getting the group to exit the room by eye/hair colour or shoe size can be an interesting variation. Have a positive lesson closure

Below are a set of rules and routines I have developed for use by lecturers with 14–16 year old learners. When establishing rules try to establish them cooperatively with students. They should be:

■ few, simple and clear

■ collaboratively constructed by all members of the school community

■ described positively and reinforced by rewarding good behaviour. Rewarding those students who behave well (walking around the room giving rewards to them) will get the majority of students on your side, which will improve the behaviour climate

■ understood by all and the reasons for them explained

■ agreed and consistently applied by all

Routines

Creating and then maintaining predictable, clear routines appropriate to your teaching area is essential.

- ■ Clear routines need to be established for:

  - ❑ entry to lesson

  - ❑ beginning of lesson

  - ❑ main body of lesson

  - ❑ end of lesson

  - ❑ exit

- ■ During the establishment phase, at the beginning of the year, time needs to be invested in establishing routines – this will save time later in the year

- ■ Halfway through the first term these routines will need reinforcing – during the Consolidation Phase. As Bill Rogers (2004: 5.2) says, 'effective teachers always maintain, consolidate and "habituate" what they establish … a progressive "habituation" regarding behaviour and learners'

- ■ Clear expectations regarding behaviour supported by clear consequences are essential

Lesson Rules and Routines

Start of the lesson

- Be punctual to lessons (lecturers should be there before students)

- Establish clear routines to settle students and to show a preparedness for the lesson. Set a target time in which students should be seated, remove outdoor clothes, get out books/planners/materials, put bags on the floor

- Try to avoid unnecessary queuing in corridors and receive students in an orderly fashion

- Discourage interruptions or queries until you have got the whole class working

- Establish a clear signal that the lesson has started – for example, countdown, click fingers

- Only start the lesson when all students are quiet and paying attention

- Ensure you have a crisp and stimulating start to your lesson

During the lesson

- Be in control and vigilant throughout the lesson

- Plan and organize the classroom and lessons to keep students interested and to minimize the opportunities for disruption

- Ensure tasks are clearly explained and supported in written form

- Develop an ability to handle the simultaneity of events – selective ignoring of some behaviour may be appropriate

End of the lesson

- Conclude with a summary of what has been learnt and give a brief overview of the content of the next lesson

- Allow sufficient time to clear away and pack up

- Ensure materials, text books are collected in and students' desks and area around them are left tidy

- Thank the class for their work and bid a friendly farewell

- For an orderly dismissal let students go a few at a time

- Most importantly, be in control during dismissal

Weekly Behaviour Management Log

Keep your own Behaviour Management Log for the first half-term. Try to add your repertoire of approaches over the duration of the log. To gain ideas, talk to a colleague or use some strategies given in this book.

Date	Subject	Session	Score How lesson went in behaviour management terms (1 = Poor, 5 = Good)	Strategies that worked	Strategies that didn't work	Next lesson I will try ... (Discuss with a colleague)

 Photocopiable: How to Manage Behaviour in Further Education
Paul Chapman Publishing 2007 © David Vizard

The importance of adapting approaches used with older students

This chapter has so far outlined strategies for lecturers to use with 14–16 year old learners in the initial phase, when we first meet them. It is important to recognize that our approaches have to be slightly modified to take account of the age and previous experiences of this group of learners. In Further Education, students are treated in a mature manner, with staff using students' first names and giving them lots of responsibilities. The ethos is very positive. Students' experiences may be very different in schools and so it is necessary to be stricter and more controlling initially with these younger learners until they can acclimatize to the college. Many students find it difficult to settle initially because college is so different.

Working with 14–16 year old learners can, however, be very worthwhile. I have had the following responses from students in speaking of their experiences in college:

■ 'It's given me confidence'

■ 'Relations with lecturers are brilliant – relaxed and positive'

■ 'I love working with people of all ages'

■ 'My life has been transformed … college has given me a real boost in life'

Key points to remember

■ Groups of students from various schools need to be brought together through team building activities

■ Making an initial impact on learners when they enter the classroom is important – a defining moment

■ Remember students will be reading you from the first moments – be aware of your body language, vocal tone and the scripts you use. They will make initial assumptions quickly. Getting the right presentation of self is essential

■ Meet and greet students as they arrive

■ Tactical pausing and use of silence (3–5 seconds gap) is a very powerful tool

■ Position is important – stand in a position where you can 'lighthouse' the group

■ Establish clear rules and routines in the first session. These should cover:

❑ entry

❑ take-up time

❑ take-up activity

❑ outlining of session

❑ transitions

❑ establishing protocols for different types of work

❑ plenary

❑ exit strategy

■ It is important to adapt the approaches you would normally use with older students to fit the background and school experience of 14–16 year olds. Also, allow them time to acclimatize to the ethos of the college

CHAPTER 4

Creating a positive learning environment

> **This chapter looks at:**
>
> ■ how to develop a positive learning environment through verbal and non-verbal communication
>
> ■ the 10 Rs of positive behaviour management: Rules, Routines, Rewards, Responsibility, Relationships, Respect, Rapport, Recognition, Rights, Resilience
>
> ■ challenges of creating a positive learning environment in workshops and practical areas
>
> ■ reward systems that actually work
>
> ■ how to create a stimulating learning environment

How to develop a positive learning environment through verbal and non-verbal communication

Some groups offer high levels of challenge and extreme behaviour and lecturers can all too easily become entrapped in a negative cycle of communication, reacting to each incident. Students soon find it is easier to get negative attention by misbehaving than attention for positive reasons. As one 15 year old I met said, 'Everyone remembers you when you do wrong. Everyone forgets you when you do right'. However, when faced with these groups of students it is extremely difficult to envisage creating a positive learning environment in which they can work. It is important to try to emphasize the positive in a ratio of five praise statements to each negative statement. Praise the students in the group who arrived punctually and brought the equipment/materials needed. Over a period of time students will discover it is more likely they will gain attention through positive behaviour than negative behaviour.

Give out nuggets of praise to learners when warranted – catch them when they are being good. Many learners in the 14–16 age group have low self-esteem due to negative experiences in life and may not have done well in the school system. To help increase their self-esteem we ought to regularly give out 'emotional small change' to the students in the form of praise. This small change will soon grow into large currency. We should always try to enhance the feelings of self-worth and competence of students by acknowledging their quality and strengths.

The way we greet students on arrival can have an influence on whether our learning environment will have a positive ethos. Standing by the door and engaging in eye contact as they arrive and talking to them, using first names and relating to their interests, is essential. This gives out the message that you are interested in them as people.

As we saw in the previous chapter, routine is important and so early on we need to establish routines such as a 2 minute take-up time on arrival to settle. Introducing a take-up activity at the beginning will help the learner to tune into the session. I use a CD with PowerPoint Starter Activities on it. This shows close-up shots of objects and pictures being exposed pixel by pixel. The students have to identify the object. Also quizzes and other activities can be used. This helps to create a positive atmosphere and focuses their attention.

When speaking to students you should be calm and use a pleasant tone. In disciplinary interventions you need to be assertive rather than aggressive. It is important to keep your own and their dignity intact. Always praise positive behaviour by naming the behaviour back to the student. When giving instructions to students or making requests it is important to be polite but not pleading. Give an instruction followed by 'Thank You', not 'I would really like it if you could do [x] as a special favour for me'.

When dealing with more difficult situations it is still possible to remain positive by using prefacing, that is, an attempt to make a praise statement before a correctional statement. For example, 'The piece of tiling that you did last session was good. However, I am a bit concerned by the lack of work this session.' When using verbal reinforcers with students they are more effective if personalized.

Being aware of our 'psychological geography' in our learning environment is important. We stand in certain positions for particular actions. We will have a point in the room where we stand to control the group and to reprimand them – the 'discipline position'. We will have a position where we will sit for informal/relaxed conversations. We will have a position we stand when we are imparting knowledge. We also may have a variety of locations when we move around the room praising students – often making use of proximity and level, usually kneeling at one side of student. At the end of the session it is important to have a relaxed ending – thanking them for their input and saying that you look forward to working with them at the next session.

Body language, in the form of non-verbal communication, can have a significant influence on the type of atmosphere we create. Sometimes if you approach a badly behaving group with trepidation and fear it will show in your body language and vocal tone. You must work on your body language to ensure this does not show. Sometimes using positive affirmations or statements can help, for example – 'this group may be challenging but I will gain experience from it'.

Sometimes lecturers sub-consciously form barrier gestures when they face groups that are poorly behaved. These barrier gestures include:

- arms folded across the chest

- standing behind a barrier such as a table

- clutching papers or books in your arms

- nervous ticks or tells that show a lack of confidence – increased blinking, rubbing neck, nose, variation in vocal tone, excessive shuffling of feet or leg movement, or excessive throat clearing

Try to adopt a relaxed position. This can be achieved by:

- using open palm gestures

- openness of arms – have a confident bearing

- asymmetrical positioning of limbs

- a sideways lean and tilt of the head

To create a positive environment non-verbally, you need to develop positive eye contact, friendly facial expressions and use of positive non-verbal communication, such as thumbs up to show agreement/pleasure. Smiling and nodding your head can show active listening.

By making effective use of silence you can allow students time to formulate answers following the asking of a question. If students make an error in their response, help them by signposting their answer, through the use of clues. To develop rapport with a student non-verbally it can on some occasions be appropriate to mirror their body language.

Reflection on practice

Think about five different ways in which you create a positive learning environment both verbally and non-verbally.

Verbally

1. _____

2. _____

3. _____

4. _____

5. _____

Non-verbally

1. _____

2. _____

3. _____

4. _____

5. _____

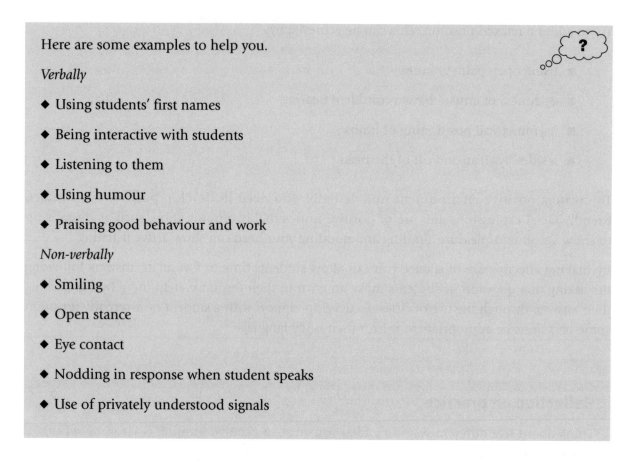

Here are some examples to help you.

Verbally

◆ Using students' first names

◆ Being interactive with students

◆ Listening to them

◆ Using humour

◆ Praising good behaviour and work

Non-verbally

◆ Smiling

◆ Open stance

◆ Eye contact

◆ Nodding in response when student speaks

◆ Use of privately understood signals

The 10 Rs of positive behaviour management

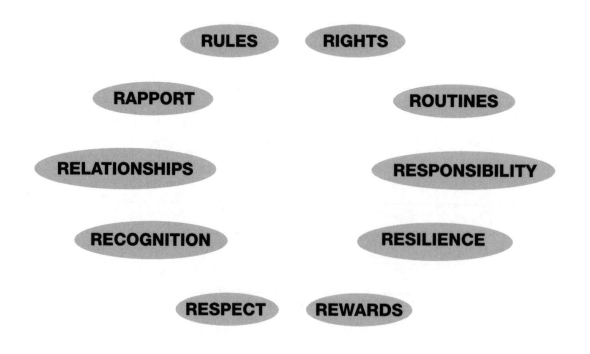

Figure 4.1 The 10 Rs of positive behaviour management

These are the ten elements that I believe are fundamental in developing a positive system of behaviour management. In the previous chapter we discussed the importance of setting up clear, mutually agreed rules and routines in the establishment phase at the beginning of the year, which take into account students' rights. The other seven Rs are listed below.

Recognition

It is important to recognize the individual differences and interests of our students. By chatting to students informally we can learn a lot about them. (Think how empowering it is to us when a line manager remembers a fact about us outside college and chats to us about it.)

Rapport

Recognizing those differences is the first step in establishing rapport with our students. Mirroring the body language of students is another good way of developing rapport. Just watch car or double glazing salespeople in action – they use body language mirroring to help develop a link with the customer. Listening to speech patterns and adopting students rate of speech and use of similar sentence lengths and vocal rhythms is useful.

Also, when a student is upset or angry, listen to the words they use when they speak. When upset, they will tend to use words relating to their sensory preferences. For example, 'I feel very upset' (kinaesthetic preference), 'I can't see the point' (visual preference). If we talk back to them framing our words in the language of their sensory preference we will connect with the student and will be able to move them from agitated state to a calmer state more quickly.

Respect

Respect is another key element of building a positive climate; if students respect a member of staff then they are less likely to pose a behaviour problem for them. Where mutually respectful exchanges take place between all members of the community then there is a positive ethos. In such communities staff:

- listen to students
- care for their opinions
- don't give up on them
- help them and take time to explain things
- make students feel special and clever
- enjoy students' company and are keen and enthusiastic about their subject
- diffuse difficult situations by allowing students to save face and avoid confrontation
- model good behaviour:

Always remember that it is easy to humiliate a young person but much harder to build up their self-esteem.

Relationships

Relationships are an important part of developing a positive climate. There is a real difference between relationships and interactions. In many settings interactions take place but relationships between staff and students are poor. Where relationships are good staff:

- learn students' names and use them

- give positive greetings – welcome students at the beginning and say farewell at the end

- remember details of their individuality

- are fair and consistent

- are patient and have a sense of humour

- are respecting and caring for students

- find time to listen to students even when they are busy

- make students feel safe and secure in class

- make allowances for students when they are having a bad day

- show mutual respect (relationships break down if a student believes that an adult doesn't like them)

- are hard but fair with discipline in students' eyes

Remember that students most in need of positive relationships are the ones more used to failing than succeeding.

Responsibility

Giving responsibility to students in any way possible is an essential part of developing a positive atmosphere. It is important to remember that responsibility grows with responsibilities, so give students responsibilities and choices. This is perhaps one of the most difficult things to achieve, but many students enjoy the extra responsibility they are given in these settings and most 14–16 year olds in Further Education talk enthusiastically and positively about their experiences. One student described their experiences to me as a 'boost in life'. Seeing students in Hospitality and Catering serving food to staff, students and members of the public, or students working with members of the public in Hair and Beauty, is always a positive experience. Students thrive on the extra responsibilities this work brings. It helps to increase their involvement and generates a sense of ownership.

Resilience

Many young people whose behaviour is challenging have extremely low levels of self-esteem. This is probably because they have had very bad experiences within education and the testing system has reinforced their negative self-image. So it is important to try to build the self-esteem and increase the resilience of learners.

Learners with low self-esteem have the following characteristics:

- negative self-image

- take few risks

- limited communication skills

- feel that they have no control over their lives

We need to build their self-esteem through the strategies outlined in this chapter. Frieman (2001) found that resilient students:

- are problem solvers

- can gain the positive attention of others

- have an optimistic view of life

- feel independent

- approach life from a proactive perspective

- feel that they have a control over their environment

- have a sense of humour

- can empathize with others

- have effective problem solving skills and coping strategies

Rewards

In developing a positive learning environment great care should be taken to ensure an appropriate system of rewards is in place. If praise is regularly given rather than the lecturer giving undue attention to negative behaviour, then the former will be seen as the best way to get the attention of the member of staff.

A myth that exists in many colleges is that older students do not like rewards and have no wish to take part in any reward schemes. In discussions with students I have found that students of all ages want to be involved in reward schemes. Involving students in developing the systems is important to help give them ownership of the scheme – such as designing stickers and certificates.

One of the best ways to reward students is not in a tangible form but through giving out those 'verbal reinforcers' and 'nuggets of praise' or through non-verbal reinforcers such as friendly facial expressions, positive eye contact and other gestures.

How to create a stimulating learning environment

To create a positive learning environment our teaching areas need to be stimulating and interesting places. However, the reality is that we may have to teach in a large number of rooms and have little control over the environment. We may also teach in workshops and practical areas that place restrictions on what we may be able to do. I believe it is important for us to get as much ownership of our spaces as possible by negotiating with other colleagues who use those spaces.

I recently visited one Leisure and Tourism room in a college in South West England which was a virtual visual feast. Inflatable sharks and dolphins were suspended from the ceiling together with an inflatable globe. Lots of bright visual materials were on the wall. Potted plants were in the corner and a poster for a feature film was on the wall with the main character expounding the values of Geography in speech bubbles (placed on the poster by the lecturer).

With over 90 per cent of the learning of students being unconscious it is important that we make the surroundings visually stimulating. We must be aware, however, that too much in the way of display, particulary if it is poorly arranged, can lead to visual clutter, which can have a negative impact.

Word Mats and Word Walls

Many rooms will have word walls and word mobiles of key terminology. I have seen A3 word mats used successfully in a number of areas. In one Sport and Leisure session a member of staff was using word mats with students. The session was dealing with muscle groups and the mats had a diagram of all of the muscles in the human body and key words associated with the groups. Students were able to highlight on the mats the different muscle groups used when exercising.

I have seen these mats used as place mats onto which students can place their work and key terminology and information is visible around the edge of the work as an *aide-mémoire*. Also many rooms have key information on how to approach activities and information on the learning cycle.

Aspirational posters

In some rooms staff will have a range of aspirational statements on display – to motivate students and help them raise their aspirations. These include:

- 'Genius is one per cent inspiration, 99 per cent perspiration' (Edison)
- 'The enemy of learning is forgetting to relax'
- 'Everyone can be more intelligent'
- 'Never stop asking Why, What, When, Where and How'
- 'I can't do it yet'
- 'Mistakes are my friends, they help me to learn'
- 'A smiling face makes a happy place'
- 'The interrogatives to use when researching a piece of work: What, When, Where, Why, How?'

Graffiti boards

In some learning environments a graffiti board is placed on the wall for students to add areas that they wish to study in a particular topic.

Joke boards

In some learning environments joke boards have been included to make the learning environments more positive. It is believed that the areas of the brain used to 'get' new jokes are the same areas used to learn a new piece of information.

Music

Playing music can be uplifting and can boost performance and intelligence in learners for short periods. Music that has 60 or less beats per minute can have a de-stressing effect. For example, the theme for the feature film *Elvira Madigan* uses a Mozart piece (Piano Concerto No. 21) that can be used for this. Students have shown a drop in blood pressure and pulse rate when listening to it. When such music is played the coordination centre of the brain is stimulated and endorphins are released and blood pressure is lowered. This will lead to decreasing levels of adrenalin in students and they will be calmer and less likely to be aggressive. Other types of music can be used with faster beats that are uplifting and motivating.

One lecturer I recently observed used a set piece of music 5–10 minutes in length when he wanted students to work quietly and independently. From an early stage his students are pre-conditioned that when they hear this piece of music they work quietly.

Acoustics and noise

External noises can disturb concentration. Wherever possible rooms should be sound-proofed against such disturbance. Buzzing lights can also interfere with concentration. Rooms need to be good acoustically, without echo effects and any reverberations. When there is a lot of external noise or where acoustics are bad students can become stressed and disengaged.

Lighting

It is important that students are able to work in well-lit environments. Working in poorly lit areas can affect a student's mood, alertness and ability to work.

Colour

The colour the walls of a room are painted can have an effect on learners. Pastel shades are particularly good at having a calming effect on students and can enhance emotions and learning as well as helping to improve concentration.

Temperature

Higher temperatures can have an effect on learners, particularly those with conditions/syndromes such as ADHD. Higher temperatures can influence neurotransmitter levels – for example, norepinephrine and serotonin. Excessive levels of these neurotransmitters can lead to increases in aggressiveness.

Re-hydration

It is important that students are able to regularly re-hydrate (see Chapter 1). We should drink about 1.2 litres of water per day. Our brains are made up of more than 80 per cent water and use 30 per cent of the water taken in by the body. Any dehydration will impact on the student's behaviour and ability to learn.

Other factors that may be considered in creating a positive learning environment are as follows.

Aromatherapy

Some colleges have used aromatherapy to create a conducive environment. Some aromatherapy oils increase concentration, reduce errors in work and improve behaviour:

- Rosemary and lemon improve memory and concentration. In Japan, 54 per cent fewer typing errors were made when these oils were used in offices

- Basil clears the mind

- Juniper stimulates the mind

Plants

Plants in a learning environment increase oxygen levels and productivity by 10 per cent. Caring for and watering plants can also have a positive effect on students.

Seating and furniture arrangement

How furniture is arranged can have a significant effect on learners. Increased physical space between learners can improve behaviour and on-task time.

Merrett and Wheldall (1990) suggest that when students were seated in rows on-task behaviour improved by 15 per cent. When reviewing individual students whose on-task behaviour had been low, there was a 30 per cent improvement in on-task behaviour.

Reflection on practice

The following pages offer some questionnaires on Physical Classroom Environment, Peripheral Learning and Positive Behaviour Management. Answer 1–10 in each set with Yes or No and score statements 11–20 on a scale of 1–5, with 1 indicating 'strongly disagree' and 5 'strongly agree'.

If you have 6 or more Yes responses to statements 1–10 and your total score for statements 11–20 is 40 or more, then you have a positive learning environment. If you have 6 or more No responses to statements 1–10 and a total score of 20 or less to statements 11–20, then you may need to reflect on practice.

Physical Environment Questionnaire

Circle YES or NO to these statements:

1	Students have access to water in my classroom.	YES/NO
2	My classroom layout promotes interaction between students and staff.	YES/NO
3	The ambience (noise/temperature/smell) promotes alertness and concentration in my classroom.	YES/NO
4	My teaching space is suitable for its purpose.	YES/NO
5	My furniture is suitably positioned for the purpose of each lesson.	YES/NO
6	My classroom supports student learning.	YES/NO
7	My classroom is well organized and purposeful.	YES/NO
8	I have control over the visual environment of my classroom.	YES/NO
9	My classroom is large enough to accommodate all groups.	YES/NO
10	The windows can be opened to provide sufficient ventilation.	YES/NO

TOTAL NUMBER OF 'YES' RESPONSES TO STATEMENTS 1–10 ......

Circle 1, 2, 3, 4 or 5 where 1 = STRONGLY DISAGREE and 5 = STRONGLY AGREE:

11	I find the use of seating plans extremely beneficial in my classroom.	1 2 3 4 5
12	My room promotes a positive climate for learning.	1 2 3 4 5
13	The furniture is comfortable and appropriately arranged.	1 2 3 4 5
14	I change the arrangement of furniture in my classroom to meet the requirements of each lesson.	1 2 3 4 5
15	The temperature in my classroom is conducive to learning.	1 2 3 4 5
16	I make very effective use of display space in my learning environment.	1 2 3 4 5
17	The level of cleanliness in my classroom is good.	1 2 3 4 5
18	There is enough equipment/materials for all students.	1 2 3 4 5
19	Displays in the classroom are appropriate to current teaching and learning.	1 2 3 4 5
20	There is sufficient natural light in my classroom.	1 2 3 4 5

TOTAL SCORE FOR RESPONSES TO STATEMENTS 11–20 ......

Peripheral Learning Questionnaire

Circle YES or NO to these statements:

1	I use aspirational posters in my classroom.	YES/NO
2	I use word walls of key terms in my classroom.	YES/NO
3	Students use suggestion/graffiti topic boards in my classroom.	YES/NO
4	I use thinking boards in my classroom where students display 'thinking style' information.	YES/NO
5	I use brain boards that show how the brain works.	YES/NO
6	I use word mats which students place under their work.	YES/NO
7	Support staff help in the development of wall displays.	YES/NO
8	I use 'thinking maps' to show connections between topic areas.	YES/NO
9	I use activities to encourage students to develop their visual sensory preference.	YES/NO
10	Students contribute to the arrangement and mounting of wall displays.	YES/NO

TOTAL NUMBER OF YES RESPONSES TO STATEMENTS 1–10   ……

Circle 1, 2, 3, 4 or 5 where 1 = STRONGLY DISAGREE and 5 = STRONGLY AGREE:

11	I regularly change displays in my classroom.	1 2 3 4 5
12	Over 50 per cent of my classroom display space is dedicated to students' work.	1 2 3 4 5
13	I encourage display areas in my room to stimulate questions from students.	1 2 3 4 5
14	Students have the opportunity to share their learning experiences with other students.	1 2 3 4 5
15	Posters on thinking and learning are displayed in my classroom.	1 2 3 4 5
16	My teaching base is a visually interesting and stimulating environment.	1 2 3 4 5
17	Use of ICT/Powerpoint promotes learning.	1 2 3 4 5
18	Rewards/achievements of students are displayed in my room.	1 2 3 4 5
19	My learning environment caters for the fact that over 90 per cent of student learning takes place unconsciously.	1 2 3 4 5
20	The visual stimulus around the college, including in the corridors, is good.	1 2 3 4 5

TOTAL SCORE FOR RESPONSES TO STATEMENTS 11–20   ……

Positive Behaviour Management Questionnaire

Circle YES or NO to these statements:

1	Students receive appropriate verbal praise.	YES/NO
2	I use good non-verbal communication to promote positive relationships.	YES/NO
3	I always keep an accurate record of rewards issued to students.	YES/NO
4	I try to encourage an environment where success is celebrated.	YES/NO
5	A strategy I use is to preface a correctional statement with a positive comment.	YES/NO
6	Students are praised for good behaviour.	YES/NO
7	I always try to give some positive comments on written feedback.	YES/NO
8	Smiling staff and students are frequently seen in school.	YES/NO
9	Peripheral learning notices accentuate the positive.	YES/NO
10	The student reward system is balanced, recognizing academic, non-academic, extra-curricular activities and service to the community.	YES/NO

TOTAL NUMBER OF YES RESPONSES TO STATEMENTS 1–10 ......

Circle 1, 2, 3, 4 or 5 where 1 = STRONGLY DISAGREE and 5 = STRONGLY AGREE:

11	All students' contributions are valued.	1 2 3 4 5
12	The reward system is clear to all staff and students.	1 2 3 4 5
13	Students were involved in the development of the system of rewards.	1 2 3 4 5
14	Students appear relaxed and motivated in all lessons.	1 2 3 4 5
15	Positive comments by the lecturer outweigh negative comments.	1 2 3 4 5
16	High quality work always results in the college recognizing this achievement by informing parents/carers.	1 2 3 4 5
17	There are enough levels in the reward system to reward high achieving students.	1 2 3 4 5
18	Rewards issued are relevant and appreciated by the target age group.	1 2 3 4 5
19	Group rewards are beneficial and help improve motivation	1 2 3 4 5
20	When correcting a student for poor behaviour I explain why the behaviour is inappropriate.	1 2 3 4 5

TOTAL SCORE FOR RESPONSES TO STATEMENTS 11–20 ......

Reward systems that actually work

Success is the lifeblood of us all – when we are successful and receive praise it makes us feel really good. Success gives a feeling of achievement and inspires students to attain higher goals. It makes them feel good about themselves and raises confidence.

The best reward systems are those in which students have an input into their development. In some colleges students have helped in the design of certificates, reward cards and stickers. This gives them ownership of the scheme.

It is also important that all sections, divisions, subject areas and staff in the institution are involved in the application of rewards.

Some schemes/systems that work include the following:

- Reward systems at their simplest level can be a recognition of a student's achievement – a record of progress and acquisition of key skills in a subject. In one Hair and Beauty area students asked the lecturer to produce a wall chart on which stickers were placed as students acquired skills.

- In another location students were given pin badges with symbols of their subject as rewards. Many students wore them with pride. These were sponsored by a local badge-making firm with which the college had links.

- In other colleges I have seen reward certificates/cards issued which are a little different. They are issued at three levels, Bronze, Silver and Gold. To make them different the Bronze Award is postcard size, the silver Award is half-postcard size and the Gold Award is postage stamp sized. Each has a different cartoon illustration, positive statements and the level on them. To add another dimension they have been made collectable by having Trump card facts on the reverse. So, for example, at each level there will be different collectable cards on a theme, either on football teams, or music, or food, or films. This makes them well sought-after items.

- Group rewards can be really motivational. In one catering area the chef uses a large pasta jar with lines drawn on it. The lines represent different levels of rewards. When individual students or the group do good work a fistful of pasta is added to the jar. If there is a problem pasta is removed. So the level can fluctuate. At the end of the week/month the level is checked and rewards issued to all members of the group. The group will often modify the behaviour of students who occasionally overstep the mark.

- Many colleges have a range of amenities that students enjoy as a part of the reward system. An example of this includes free beauty treatments, free hair makeover, free meals in college restaurants.

- In some locations I have seen lecturers issue Teaching and Learning banknotes of varying unitary value. These are issued when students complete key components of modules. These notes can then be exchanged for reward items, such as stationery items including pens from the college shop.

- Putting fluorescent card stars into a box with a student's name on as a reward is another system used. At the end of a given period the stars are counted up and the student with the most stars will gain a reward. Rewards could be issued to all students with stars in the box, at varying levels depending on the number of stars they have gained.

- A Building and Construction lecturer in one college uses Golden Time with his learners. As components of a session are completed students build up units of Golden Time. This can then be cashed in later. In this context the units count towards time in the Sports Hall to play lunchtime soccer which he referees.

- In a number of E2E schemes (Entry to Employment) students who have re-engaged with education are rewarded for completing sections of their modules: completing 50 per cent of module – CD voucher is available; completing 75 per cent of module – cinema tickets given; completing 100 per cent of module – £35 cash is available.

- Many colleges have 'Student of the week' in different subject areas. Their photo is displayed and, as in many jobs, a badge is worn. In newsletters their achievements and rewards are recognized. For many students the appreciation of lecturers and peers is important.

- Some colleges hold termly award ceremonies where students receive a variety of awards for their work.

- Other colleges, to celebrate rights of passage, will generate Year Books or CDs/DVDS of all the achievements of students in a photographic/video form.

Challenges of creating a positive learning environment in workshops and practical areas

In many practical areas there are a large number of Health and Safety factors to consider and this can have an impact on work. Often peripheral learning notices may be restricted and in some areas not allowed. Also a range of staff may share use of the workshops and practical areas, so ownership of the space may be a challenge. There is little to no flexibility in movement of equipment and altering workspaces because many are fixed. Many of the areas have to have strict rules relating to the use of items – hot pans, ovens, ramps, jacks, guillotines and blow torches.

There is a challenge also because many of the younger learners find it difficult to conform to the specialist protective clothing and items they have to wear. Examples include eye and ear protectors, protective clothing including hard capped boots and hair covering. Another impediment can be students having to provide the right equipment/tools. We need to build as positive a learning environment as we can using many of the strategies outlined in this chapter. Working in classrooms for the theory/portfolio work can allow you to fully implement strategies.

Key points to remember

- Try to make positive statements in a proportion of five positive to each negative statement

- Give out 'emotional small change' to learners to boost self-esteem

- Meet and greet students on arrival at your room

- Rules and routines need to be established early

- Be polite but not pleading

- Make verbal reinforcers positive by using first names

- Body language and vocal tone/command account for over 90 per cent of communication

- Use open not closed body language; assume a relaxed position

- Be aware of your 'psycho-geography'

- Use positive non-verbal cues

- Make effective use of silence

- Remember the 10 Rs of positive behaviour management

- Create a stimulating learning environment: remember the importance of:

  - ☐ Peripheral learning notices: including word mats, word walls and aspirational posters

  - ☐ Music

  - ☐ Room acoustics

  - ☐ Lighting

  - ☐ Colour

  - ☐ Temperature

  - ☐ Re-hydration

  - ☐ Aromatherapy

  - ☐ Plants

  - ☐ Seating and furniture arrangement

- Develop a range of rewards for learners. Remember the importance of how we create a positive learning environment both verbally and non-verbally

- In practical areas and workshops it is important to develop a range of positive learning notices and strategies after considering Health and Safety issues

CHAPTER 5

Effective strategies to use with students displaying challenging behaviour

This chapter looks at:

■ effective scripts/phrases used to manage behaviour

■ applying sanctions in a consistent manner

■ appropriate sanctions that can be applied – given that many students in the 14–16 age group are only in college a short time each week

■ practical strategies and interventions to use with students

In dealing with students, particularly badly behaved students, it is important to think carefully about the words we use – an incorrect phrase or wrongly chosen word can fan the flames of adolescent discontent. It is important to develop scripts that can clearly get our message across and be unambiguous. Also the way that a message is presented in vocal tone and in conjunction with our body language can impact on how the message is received. An aggressive tone and intimidatory body language can cause problems.

Effective scripts/phrases used to manage behaviour

■ The way we greet students on arrival can have a real impact on the way the session goes. Standing by the door and welcoming students as they arrive is a good strategy. The greeting should show a recognition of them as individuals

■ How we dismiss the students at the end of the lesson is important. Be positive, issue any rewards, thank them for their work and say that you are looking forward to working with them in the next lesson

■ Use of appropriate humour is important – it can lighten the atmosphere

■ At every opportunity we need to give out emotional small change to students: 'Catch 'em being good'. We can never give enough praise. Give out nuggets of praise

- Remember that 'courtesy is contagious'

- Acknowledge students who are getting it right

- These strategies can create a positive atmosphere where being recognized for good work and behaviour is commonplace. Bad behaviour becomes a less attractive option

Vocal Tone, Pitch, Pace and Posture

Tone

- Be assertive not aggressive. Practise making your voice sound more commanding and strong. A confident tone is important to adopt

- Make your point through varying the tone of your voice. Be aware of the situation, sometimes a calming tone may be best

Posture and voice

- Be relaxed, an upright posture will help project your voice. If you are slumped, your voice could sound strained. Use body language that conveys authority

- Control your breathing. Efficient breathing is important in voice control

- Speak slowly and clearly – avoid slurring/losing endings of words. Articulating sounds will help you sound more decisive and authoritative

- Try to vary the volume to match the circumstances

Pace and pause

- On average we speak at about 125 words per minute when speaking in public. Speaking quicker than this may give the impression of being too nervous

- Varying pace can help us to communicate more effectively and keep the attention of students. However avoid speaking too much and too quickly – keep your message short and simple

Pitch

- Most of us have a pitch range of about two octaves, with men's pitch range lower than women's because of vocal chord length

- People make assumptions about a person from the pitch of their voice. A low-pitched voice can give the impression of control and authority, where a higher pitched voice may appear emotional or a soft target for misbehaving students

Scripts

- ■ When giving instructions to students or managing their behaviour we need to ensure we have a clear script to use. Practise the following:

  - ❏ Describe what you want them to do rather than what not to do. For example, say 'stop what you are doing, face this way and listen'. Just think of your reaction when you are told not to do something – most of us are tempted to do it

  - ❏ Focus on the required behaviour – sanction the behaviour not the student

  - ❏ Staying solution-focused is a good strategy to employ – 'We're in this together, let's try to find a solution'

  - ❏ Validating a student's feelings can be useful – 'I can see you are upset'

  - ❏ When giving instructions to a student make sure it is followed by a 'thank you'. It makes us sound as if we expect compliance

  - ❏ Moving around the room giving quiet instructions or comments in a low key manner is a good way of gaining compliance

  - ❏ Avoid pleading and weak words

  - ❏ Try to avoid over-verbalising – we can say too much and as a result our message is weakened

  - ❏ Stay in control by initiating and ending interactions with students. However try to avoid point-scoring with students. It may be best to ignore some comments. Be 'Teflon' coated – nothing sticks

  - ❏ Having made a comment, give the student take-up time to comply. This is particularly important with an angry child

  - ❏ Use naming the rule, where we identify what we want – 'sitting quietly please … thanks'

  - ❏ Do not back students into a corner. Give them options. Allow them to save face – 'there are two ways that the situation can go, the rules say [x] and the reason for this rule is [x]. Ignore it and the consequence is likely to be [x], however there is another way you could go [x], which will have positive outcomes'

  - ❏ Give students direct choices based on the rules. For example, a student is chewing gum: take the bin to the student and say 'You can keep your break by putting the gum in the bin. Or you can keep the gum and lose break. You decide.' When they conform say, 'Good choice'

  - ❏ Giving all staff a choices script to use with students can be helpful – 'Let's be very clear about this. As a member of staff at this college I am instructing you to [x]. You now have a choice. Either cooperate fully and follow my instructions or, if you choose not to, there will be a consequence of [x]'. If the student follows the instructions say 'thank you for making the right choice'. If not, then say 'You have chosen to refuse my direct instruction. The consequence of your choice is that your parents will be informed of your refusal and you may be sent home or excluded.' The script should be delivered slowly and calmly to allow the student take-up time and also time to calm down

❏ Maybes/partial agreement – this can help you to take the heat out of a situation. A script for partial agreement could be:

Student:	He gave me a dirty look.
Lecturer:	Maybe he did but I would really like you to [x]
Student:	Why have you got lines all over your face?
Lecturer:	Maybe I have but [x]
Student:	You are a bad lecturer
Lecturer:	Maybe I am but [x]

❏ Students when challenged about their poor behaviour try to divert the lecturer's attention from the primary behaviour by smoke screening. This can be done by sulking, looking away from you and making all manner of gestures. If caught doing something, they may deny they did it or that the person next to them started it. They may suggest that you are always picking on them or that you let others get away with it or that another colleague lets them do it. In these circumstances tactically ignore the behaviour. Avoid arguing and focus on the primary behaviour. Block out their comments. Do not respond to them. Use the 'broken record' technique of repeating the same line – 'I am referring to you and how you hit George'. If used with command in your voice it is a powerful tool

❏ Smile therapy is a good approach

❏ When students say other negative things towards you, do not show that you are phased by their comments. Thank them for their criticism:

Student:	You have got sweat marks on your jacket.
Lecturer:	Thanks for pointing that out. I will put a different one on tomorrow. Now continue with your work for now. Thank you.

❏ When re-directing a student who is not conforming it may be necessary to use single and double What's.

Single What:

Lecturer:	What's the rule for when you want to ask a question?
	[Pause – await student response]
Lecturer:	Use it.
	[Pause]
Lecturer:	Thank you.

Double What

Lecturer: What are you doing and what should you be doing now?

                    [Pause – await student response]

Lecturer: Go and do it.

                    [Pause]

Lecturer: Thank you.

When/Then:

Lecturer: It's a shame when you shout out because then I can't hear other students' opinions. When you put your hand up I will listen to your opinion.

❏ A more direct approach may be to use direct rule statements: 'We've got a rule for asking questions and I expect you to use it. Thanks.'

❏ When issuing a consequence it needs to be one that:

– is related to the deed (dropping litter, the consequence is clearing litter)

– has reasonableness – certainty not severity. If you say a sanction will be applied, ensure that it is. It doesn't have to be a big sanction – just detaining students for a few minutes at the end of the session is normally enough. Students do not respect staff who threaten students often but do not issue sanctions

– keeps your own and their respect intact; do not hurt or humiliate

– allows time to try to repair and rebuild at the end and separate amicably; festering feuds and grudges do not get us anywhere

– avoids backing yourself into a corner. Some scripts we use can lead to stalemate, for example:

Lecturer: Why haven't you brought your work book?

Student: Because I've lost it (in a dismissive tone)

Lecturer: How dare you be so rude

Student: 'I didn't do anything. You've got it in for me'

The likely result is out and out confrontation. There is little 'wriggle room' for the lecturer. Perhaps giving the student paper to use and asking them at the end of the session to have a good look for the book at home would avoid this confrontation. If they can't find it, then they can buy a new one next session.

Applying sanctions in a consistent manner

It is important that sanctions are applied in a consistent manner. Some of the most challenging students like to work in an environment where there are firm consistent boundaries. Learners do not like it when students are treated differently for the same misdemeanour so it is important that we get staff teams dealing with 14–16 year old learners to work consistently and apply sanctions in a consistent manner. In Chapter 9 I suggest ways to develop a consistency model for staff.

Appropriate sanctions that can be applied

Given that many students in the 14–16 age group are only in college a short time each week:

- Remember sanctions limit behaviour – rewards will quickly change students behaviour

- Try to keep reprimands private and only audible to students being reprimanded. This does not give the student the 'oxygen of publicity' that they were seeking from their peer group. When you use low volume as opposed to high volume then the frequency of disruptive behaviour is likely to decline

- If you are unfair and embarrass a student they will feel the comments are unreasonable and that they have lost face in front of their peer group and they may well retaliate

- When working with students don't back them into a corner – giving partial agreement can help to reduce conflict

- Differentiate the serious from the trivial. It is sometimes best to tactically ignore the trivial

- When dealing with an incident try to avoid disturbing the rest of the class

- Do not show fear

- Sometimes we get lost in the heat of the emotional moment:

  - Describe behaviour

  - Do not make it personal

  - Give the student the right to reply for all but the most serious misdemeanours

- Tune into how the student is feeling before choosing from your repertoire

- If you reprimand a student held in high esteem in the group and the behaviour is checked, then the ripple effect is strong and good for the lecturer

- When dealing with an incident leave students' previous bad behaviour behind. Respond to the here and now

- It is pointless to enforce a consequence in the heat of the emotional moment when the student is too upset or angry. Student and lecturer may need cool-off time to calm down and settle before the situation can be reviewed. It is all too easy for both parties to get lost in their behaviour

- Commands should be decisive and warm

- As in a football match good referees, when cautioning a player, often get them to move towards them rather than them going to the player, the same should be done when reprimanding challenging students

- Students who are challenging will try to blame everyone for their poor behaviour – the lecturer, parents or other students. Deflect the responsibility for their behaviour back to the student. Get them to understand that they own their behaviour and they can change the consequence by choosing to modify their behaviour

- Once you have dealt with the situation get the focus of the individual back to the main focus of the lesson

Many 14–16 year old students are only in college for a day or part of a day per week currently. This makes follow-up to any issues difficult to achieve. Application of sanctions can also be difficult. It is therefore important that clear lines of communication exist between college and schools. Information exchange to deal with incidents and offer support in follow-up needs to be achieved. For small incidents immediate detention of the learner at the end of session may be quite effective. Remember it is the certainty not the severity that is important in relation to sanctioning.

Practical strategies/interventions to use with students

When dealing with students displaying challenging behaviour the following points are important to remember.

- Avoid 'Venus Fly Trap' moments – getting drawn into a situation. It is easy to get involved in a power struggle. Make it clear you are not coming out to play. Be objective and keep your responses low key

- Keep to the point – do not let the classroom disruptors win, act early to avoid escalation. In your interactions be brief and positive

- The learner may argue and blame you and others for the incident. We need to refocus them by getting in their line of sight and blocking their comments by using open palms. Say 'No' in a firm voice and reiterate the behaviour that was inappropriate, giving them a clear choice:

Lecturer: You may wish to continue to behave in that way. If you do, you know the likely consequence.

You may choose an alternative way.

[Leave time to reflect]

- Many students have spent their lives gaining negative attention by poor behaviour. When they fail to gain attention they become more and more outrageous in their behaviour

- Create a clarity when you are giving instructions

- Make your expectations clear to learners – outline what you expect in relation to punctuality, entry to room, take-up time, equipment requirements, working noise levels, movement around rooms, exit strategies

- Immediate intervention such as moving a student to a different desk or using 'Time Out' where they spend time away in an area set up by college, to reflect

- Standing next to the student and asking if they might like help might get the student back on task and remove the need for a sanction

- Standing behind them and saying nothing is also powerful – speaking would weaken the effect

- Writing names on the board – if a student's name has been written three times by the end of the lesson then a sanction would be applied

- If you threaten a sanction you must carry it out. Students have least respect for staff who threaten punishments often but never give them. What you say you must do. Don't make disproportionate and unrealistic threats in the heat of the moment

- The sanction could be as little as detaining the student for a few minutes

- Detaining students works best when the lesson backs onto a break

- The sanctions students least like are losing social time or if parents are contacted

---

Key points to remember

- Remember the importance of tone, posture and voice, pace and pause, and pitch when dealing with students displaying challenging behaviour

- Having scripts prepared to respond to particular types of poor behaviour is important:

  ❑ Describe what you want rather than what you do not want

  ❑ Be solution-focused

  ❑ Be assertive – avoid pleading

  ❑ Do not over-verbalize

  ❑ Stay in control

  ❑ Give students take-up time to comply with instruction

- Try to manage behaviour and apply sanctions in a consistent manner

■ When applying sanctions remember:

❏ Keep reprimands private

❏ Certainty not severity

❏ Tune in to how the student is feeling

❏ Leave students' previous bad behaviour behind

❏ Avoid getting drawn into their behaviour – avoid a power struggle

❏ Be clear in your instruction – avoid emotional languag

CHAPTER 6

The importance of body language

This chapter looks at:

In this chapter we will look at the importance of body language in communication and the key elements of body language to use for effective management of behaviour. These will include:

■ Importance of the 4 Cs: Clusters, Congruence, Context, and Culture

■ eye contact

■ positioning

■ posture

■ facial expressions

■ non-verbal cueing

■ different types of body language and their meanings

■ barrier position

■ tell-tale signs of liars

■ non-verbal communication that indicates when someone is becoming angry

■ relaxed position

■ rapport building

■ vocal tone, pitch and pace

■ use of silence

Non-verbal communication provides clues to how people think and feel. (Ribbens and Thompson, 2001)

In Chapter 4 we discussed how we might develop a positive learning environment through non-verbal communication. In this chapter we will look at how we can use body language to successfully manage behaviour. A key tool in our locker when managing badly behaving students is an understanding of body language. The body language we display will have a real impact on how successful we are in managing behaviour. If we are talking tough, does our body language confirm or contradict this? Is there a congruence between our verbal and non-verbal communication? We can also read the body language in students to provide us with clues to show us what they are really thinking.

Body language contributes a great deal to how we communicate. According to Mehrabian (1981), 7 per cent of any message is conveyed in the words spoken, 38 per cent in paralanguage/vocal tone and 55 per cent of our message communicated through a non-verbal form. Body language betrays emotion or thought and is delivered and read unconsciously. There is a need to analyse how we appear when we are involved in a disciplinary interaction with students. Sometimes by rehearsing response in front of a mirror or into a video camera we can easily analyse body language and review how we convey a message.

The importance of the 4 Cs

Based on work by Pease (2000: 14–16) and my experience in the classroom, in looking at body language we need to remember the 4Cs (Vizard, 2004b):

- Clusters

- Congruence

- Context

- Culture

Clusters

Reading too much into a single piece of body language is a mistake. A little knowledge can be a dangerous thing. Also there can be several interpretations of the same type of body language. Look for clusters of body language that have the same meaning and interpretation. For example, if their Adam's Apple is jumping, their ankles are locked and shoulders are hunched, then this could be a sign of apprehension and anxiety.

Congruence

Look for congruence between verbal and non-verbal communication. For example, uncertainty in voice, together with rubbing of eyes and nose may convey that the person is lying.

Context

Some non-verbal communication occurs in direct relationship to the context in which an individual finds themselves. Someone sitting with arms and legs crossed and looking down could be interpreted as a negative pose but in reality this could be someone in a room where the air-conditioning is set at too low a temperature and the pose is to avoid the onset of frost-bite!

Culture

As a television advert for a bank told us a few years ago, remember the same gesture will mean different things to people in different parts of the world.

In some cultures:

- Smiling is a startle response to being told off

- Staring at someone is the most disrespectful thing you could do

- Standing close to someone is a natural response when feeling guilty.

Some of the key areas relating to non-verbal communication are discussed below.

Eye contact

In elicitating the strategies used by successful staff one key area relates to eye contact.

- Using eye contact can engage attention, display our interest and also indicate intent

- When initially meeting and greeting students at the classroom doorway at the beginning of each lesson we need to have firm eye contact with them

- At the start of the lesson we need to scan the whole group. Using eye contact can engage student attention and will indicate your awareness of all students. You should also engage in longer eye contact with students who are the influencers in the group. However, avoid staring too much as it can create a perception of hostility or threat

- Do not give off any frightened or passive messages. For example, staring into the distance, looking at the ground. This eye dip movement is a submissive gesture

- Avoid the eye shuttle where you flick your eyes from side to side without head movement. This is a startle response and also a submissive gesture, where a person is taking in everything happening around them and can appear as though they are looking for escape routes

- When moving around the room a sideways glance towards a student can be controlling as it will generate an attitude of doubt or suspicion

■ If a student is misbehaving get into the student's line of sight and establish eye contact with a stare (by doing this you will establish a clear message that you expect the student to change their behaviour). Give your direction and then move away to allow them take-up time to conform. In these circumstances try to avoid unnecessary extended eye contact

■ Remember that people in conversation look at each other between 40 and 75 per cent of the time, according to Ribbens and Thompson (2002: 13). Any longer than that can be seen as unsettling, embarrassing or threatening. A longer stare may be needed with some students. When talking we maintain eye contact for 40 per cent of the time, we have to glance away to think of the next point. When listening we engage in eye contact for over 75 per cent of the time, according to Ribbens and Thompson (2002: 13). Moving around the room and moving into student space with a look is effective in managing behaviour for 90 per cent of the time

■ To show approval it is important when talking to student not to gaze off, look at paperwork or look at your watch. These non-verbal cues show dislike or disagreement

Positioning

During opening of lesson

■ When speaking to the class stand in a position where you can scan or 'lighthouse' the whole group

■ It is important psychologically for you to be able to see the whole group

■ Think about your power position. This relates to whether you are left- or right-handed. Right-handed lecturers are normally right-eye dominant and would be in their 'power position' if they stood in a position in the room where they could scan the room from left to right (see Figure 6.1)

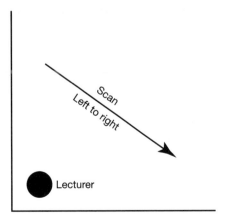

Figure 6.1 Left to right scanning

- Left-handed lecturers are normally left-eye dominant and would be in their 'power position' if they stood in a position in the room where they could scan the room from right to left (see Figure 6.2)

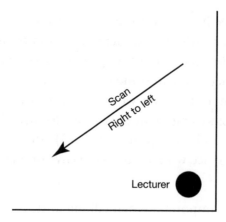

Figure 6.2 Right to left scanning

- Some students are aware that lecturers can sometimes have a blindspot just to their right if left-eye dominant or to their left if right-eye dominant. Some challenging students are aware of this and can gravitate to those areas

- It is important to remember the 'psychological geography' mentioned in Chapter 4

Patrolling

- It is essential that you patrol your territory frequently – you should avoid having no-go areas in your learning environment. Visit all areas of the room

- When settling a group when they begin to work it may be best to patrol your classroom moving around the perimeter of the room. This will keep the maximum number of students in your gaze whilst they are settling into their task

- A good position to stand is at the back of the room for periods of time. The students, without the aid of wing mirrors on their desks are put at a psychological disadvantage

Proximity

- When teaching it may be necessary to move around the room and move into areas where problem behaviours may be developing. Going towards a student and putting your hand on their desk but without stopping talking to the group can have a powerful effect

■ If notes are being passed around, stand next to the student holding the note and say nothing. The likely outcome is that the note will be put away

■ Standing behind a student who is not working, slightly within their personal space bubble but without saying anything, can be powerful

■ Regarding physical closeness, Pease (2000: 20–21), based on work by Hall, 1959 suggested that each individual has a personal space bubble of 46 cm – the 'intimate zone'. If anyone goes inside of this space we can feel threatened. When a person becomes angry, the boundary of this space is likely to increase, so it is important when dealing with students that we do not appear to be invading their personal space bubble, which might provoke confrontation

Level

■ Standing over a student whilst they are seated can put you at a psychological advantage but it is probably better to avoid this as it can be very intimidating. Sitting at the same level, or even better crouching at a slightly lower level, can lead to more effective communication and reduce the likelihood of increasing conflict.

Posture

■ Posture is very important, and so try to stand upright with a straight back when working with a class of students during the formal parts of the lesson and when dealing with disciplinary matters. Avoid at all costs standing and stooping slightly with your head down and leg bent as it creates an impression of a lack of confidence

■ Standing with your feet slightly apart is a confident posture. A closed gait can show lack of confidence

■ Stand with an open posture. Avoid closed body language, such as folded arms

Bodily orientation

The angle and direction in which your body points is said to indicate your feelings. If you point away from the person it could be perceived that you have a negative attitude towards them. In conflict situations it is important to avoid standing face to face as this can inflame the conflict. It is best to stand at right angles to the person in these situations. However, in some situations it is best to stand leaning slightly forward and square on to make more of your stature.

Head lowering or tilting

Submissive people frequently lower their head or tilt it to one side. It is a sign of appeasement and we should try to avoid such movements with students

Facial expressions

Our faces are mirrors to our minds. (Roffey, 2004)

Collett (2004: 54–57) suggested we all have certain 'ticks and tells' that can give away what we are thinking. These include the following.

- Frowning and the raising of eyebrows indicate disapproval. Shaking or nodding of the head are ways to indicate disapproval or approval, respectively

- Increased blinking is a sign of anxiety. When our mind is aroused or it is racing there is an increase in the normal blink rate. 'Our normal blinking rate is about 20 blinks per minute, but it can increase to four or five times that figure when we feel under pressure' (Collett, 2004: 290)

- A narrowing of the eyes is also a signal of control or dominance. Narrowing the eyes gives the impression the person is looking through the slit in their helmet. Clint Eastwood, in the 'Dollar' series of movies, used this expression frequently

- Lowering of the eyebrows gives the impression of dominance because it creates a more confrontational stare (when we are angry we tend to lower our eyebrows)

- Raising of eyebrows, as well as signalling disapproval, can also indicate submissiveness

- If the mouth is set into a resolute position without smiling this can be very controlling – the horizontal mouth shape. Symmetrical smiles are seen as sincere. Asymmetrical smiles are seen as insincere

- To raise the head and push the bottom teeth beyond the top set is seen as a common gesture of defiance or control used in confrontation. The 'jaw thrust' is also a sign of dominance

Non-verbal cueing

You can practise a range of non-verbal cues to give to students. These carry a clear unspoken message, direction or reminder. These will save lesson disruption and will save your voice. Lecturers in practical areas are particularly effective in using non-verbal cues in their voice-sapping teaching environments.

We all use a range of non-verbal cues with students and some of the best examples are those used by learning support workers when they signal to students across the room non-verbally. In the slightest movement of the hand, tilt of the head or facial expression they can signal their wishes or responses to the student. In workshops and practical areas, a repertoire of non-verbal cues is essential.

Some cues of this type would include:

- Smiling and nodding in response to a student – shows an interest and approval

- Walking towards student when they are talking – indicates interest

- Finger wagging – admonishment

- Raised first finger – to gain attention

- Thumbs up or down – good or bad behaviour

- Finger to lips – request for quiet

- Palms of hands facing and moving downwards – quieten down

- Finger pointing downwards – sit down

- Four fingers pointing downwards – sit on all four legs of chair

- Hands moving away from top of head – remove hat

- Pointing to watch – take-up time over and time now being wasted

- Shaking/nodding – showing disapproval/approval

- Clicking fingers/clapping hands – to get attention of group

- Holding arm in the air – students in turn do the same to show they are ready

- Rotating hands – hurry up

In our consideration of non-verbal cueing, both here and in the rest of this chapter, we need to be aware that some students with certain conditions and syndromes – for example those on the autistic spectrum – will not find it easy to decode non-verbal communication in others. They may not be able to interpret your gestures so utilizing these strategies with these students may meet with limited success.

Reflection on practice

Think about the range of non-verbal cues you use with students. List the cues and give each a score on their effectiveness: score 1 for not very effective and score 5 for those that are very effective.

Compare your scores with another member of staff and work out your own Top 5 of the most effective non-verbal cues.

Our Top 5

1. _____

_____

2. _____

_____

3. _____

_____

4. _____

_____

5. _____

_____

Different types of body language and their meanings

- **Palm down:** Confidence, assertiveness and dominance

- **Brisk, erect walk:** Confidence

- **Sitting with hands clasped, behind head, legs crossed:** Confidence, superiority

- **Clearing throat:** Sign of doubt, disagreement. Excessive use can be a sign of deception or desire

- **Adam's Apple jumping:** Unconscious sign of anxiety

- **Arms crossed on chest:** Defensiveness

- **Locked ankles:** Apprehension

- **Biting nails:** Insecurity, nervousness

- **Gaze off:** Dislike or disagreement

- **Looking down, face turned away:** Disbelief

- **Touching, slightly rubbing nose:** Rejection, doubt, lying

- **Rubbing the eye:** Doubt, disbelief

- **Patting/fondling hair:** Lack of self-confidence, insecurity

- **Pulling or tugging at ear:** Indecision

- **Standing with hands on hips:** Readiness, aggression

- **Hands clasped behind back:** Anger, frustration, apprehension

- **Tapping or drumming fingers:** Impatience

- **Sitting with hands on hips:** Readiness, aggression

- **Gaze down:** Defeated attitude, guilt or shame

- **Walking with hands in pockets, shoulders hunched:** Dejection

- **Hand to cheek:** Evaluation, thinking

- **Pinching bridge of nose, eyes closed:** Negative evaluation

- **Stroking chin:** Trying to make a decision

- **Sitting with legs crossed, foot kicking slightly:** Boredom

- **Head resting in hand, eyes downcast:** Boredom

- **Rubbing hands:** Anticipation

- **Tilted head:** Interest

Barrier positions

Barrier gestures can be unhelpful when dealing with challenging students. Some examples of barrier gestures include:

- folded or crossed arms, which show defensiveness or hostility

- having one arm across the body, which shows nervousness or lack of self-confidence

- holding books or a bag in front of you as a barrier, which shows nervousness and defensiveness

Tell-tale signs of a liar

It is also useful when dealing with badly behaving students to be able to detect any lies that may be told.

The ticks or tells that a liar may display include:

- Making odd facial expressions

- Grinding teeth or biting lips

- Increased blinking/rubbing of eyes – because liars try to keep their eyes fixed on you. They know that liars supposedly can not look people in the eye. Also they need to monitor how their story is coming across in case they need to modify their approach. They do this by looking closely at the listener. In consequence eyes become drier and itchy – hence the blinking and rubbing of eyes

■ Rubbing of nose – increased blood flow around the eyes when lying leads to increased blood pressure and so the nose grows imperceptibly and a hormone is secreted, which leads to hairs in the nostrils itching

■ Scratching hairs on neck – again, this is due to increased blood flow

■ Right/left eye movement – according to Pease and Pease (2002: 285), 'when most right-handed people are recalling an event that actually happened they engage their left brain and look to the right. When inventing a story they engage their right brain and look to the left'. In the case of left-handed people when they are inventing a story they look to the right. This is illustrated in Figure 6.3

	Lie	Truth
Right-handed people	Look to left	Look to right
Left-handed people	Look to right	Look to left

Figure 6.3 Truth and lie table (based on Pease and Pease, 2002)

■ Speech errors

■ Alteration in pitch of voice

■ Excessive throat clearing

■ Adam's Apple jumping

■ Smiling

   ❑ fast and symmetrical – sincere smile

   ❑ slow and asymmetrical or crooked – insincere smile. This occurs because people are trying to show an emotion they don't feel

■ Hands/fingers over the mouth – the source of the lie, the mouth, is covered; the younger the person, the more obvious they make it

■ Taking longer to answer questions

■ Suddenly the person starts to make fewer gestures – to avoid any chance of detection

■ There is a lot of non-verbal leakage, for example, the person's upper body shows few ticks or tells but their feet and legs will move a lot. There is a lot of fidgeting and involuntary movements – the micro-tells

■ Micro-tells (Collett, 2004) – the body controls most body language when a person is telling a lie but sometimes an involuntary piece of body language may be glimpsed that reveals true feelings. Spotting these brief and subtle changes is the key to unmasking a liar

Non-verbal communication that indicates when someone is becoming angry

- A look of agitation and becoming fidgety

- Contorted face

- Facial colour changes – it deepens and then goes pale

- Expressionless or angry gaze

- Dilated pupils

- Eyes wide open and bulging

- Hostile eye contact

- Breathing faster

- Perspiring

- Speaking louder and faster

- Moving more quickly

- Tense muscles

- Hunched shoulders

- Leaning forward, fists clenched, tight facial expression

- Upright stance and threatening

- Thrusting head and chin forward

- Easily distracted and non-focused

- Pacing around

- Looking away

- Aggressive gesturing with pointed fingers

- Standing face to face

Relaxed position

Try to appear relaxed when faced with difficult students. Students will be trying to get a reaction from you by trying to identify your 'hot buttons'. They will be reading your body language closely. Try to appear relaxed by:

- asymmetrical positioning of limbs

- an openness of arm position

- using open palm gestures

- use of sideways lean and tilt of the head

- adopting a more reclining position when seated

Rapport building

When dealing with angry and badly behaving students it is important to think how to develop a rapport with them.

- Angry students will speak using words of their sensory preference. Listen and mirror the language of their sensory preference back to them. For example: 'I can't see the point' – the student has a visual sensory preference so I would reply in a visual language, 'Lets look at it again.' A student with an auditory sensort preference might say, 'I am frustrated because you are not listening to me.' So my response might be, 'I hear what you have said' – then paraphrase some of the things the student has just said. A student with a kinaesthetic sensory preference might say, 'It feels like nobody likes me in this group.' My response might be, 'Hang on a minute' – followed by examples of where the lecturer and students have been supportive of them.

- Try to mirror their actions and then the other person will unconsciously feel a sense of connection with you

- Listen to their speech patterns and try to adopt their rate of speech, using similar intonations and rhythms

- Use similar sentence length and colloquialisms

- Practise Interactional Synchronizing, whereby you move in a similar way

- Mirroring their body language will also develop a rapport, although with some students you may not wish to mirror their body language

- Adopting a similar breathing pattern is another technique that can be used

Once you have tuned in to the student's emotional state and matched it, you are in a position to change their mood. You should change your behaviour to lead them slightly in the direction that you would like them to move.

Vocal tone, pitch and pace

- Be assertive rather than aggressive. Practise making your voice sound more commanding and strong

- Try to keep a confident tone

- Make your point by raising or lowering your voice

- Speaking in a lower tone can give you more authority. Some politicians have had vocal coaching to enable them to speak in a lower tone

- Try to speak in a calming tone – 'Calm words, calm children'

- A relaxed upright posture is essential to present your voice in its best condition

- Make your message clear – don't try to make too many points at once as this can weaken your message

- Speak clearly – don't slur your words or lose word endings

- Articulate sounds that will make you more decisive and authoritative

- Try to vary your volume to match the circumstance

- Check the speed and rhythm of your speech. Speaking too quickly may give the impression of being too nervous

- Try to avoid pleading statements

Use of silence

Silence is a very powerful tool in your behaviour management toolbox. Think of the dramatic effect in a theatre when an actor uses silence – the same will occur in disciplinary interactions.

- If you ask for silence, wait until you get it. Talking over student chatter will severely undermine your authority. Use of a stopwatch to record time to be made up while you wait will stop the noise once one detention has been given

- When we start a lesson or are about to be involved in a disciplinary interaction with students it is important that we wait for silence. The same wait for silence should be observed when we bring students together during the lesson and before their dismissal at the end

- When giving a command or becoming involved in a disciplinary interaction, tactical pausing is a good strategy to use. Use student's first name – pause for up to 5 seconds – then make your statement. In the tactical pause it is essential that you maintain eye contact

- Moving into the student's territory and standing behind them and saying nothing can be used to indicate to the student that he or she has been noticed

- If there is poor behaviour look at the student in silence as this can be unnerving for them

- Sometimes it will be necessary to tactically ignore some minor incidents of poor behaviour because responding to every incident, no matter how minor, can be extremely disruptive

- If a student makes an inappropriate/disruptive comment, silence can be as effective in indicating to the student that he/she is not behaving appropriately as a verbal reprimand would be

Key points to remember

- Importance of the 4 Cs – Clusters, Congruence, Context and Culture

- Posture – ensure you stand upright and avoid closed body language

- Avoid barriers – standing behind a desk/holding books to chest

- Eye contact – sustain firm eye contact with students

- Positioning – when teaching stand in a position where you can scan the whole group. Stand in your 'power position' – related to eye dominance

- Patrol your area

    ❏ Do not have no-go areas

    ❏ On occasions standing at the back of the room is good

- Proximity

    ❏ Move around the room and stand close to those misbehaving

    ❏ Try not to invade the 46 cm personal space bubble

- Level – your interactions may be more successful if you crouch or kneel next to the student; standing over a seated student appears to be controlling

- Bodily orientation – the angle and direction your body points will indicate your feelings

- Facial expressions – lowering eyebrows, narrowing eyes, jaw thrusts and horizontal mouth shape are examples of controlling expressions

- Non-verbal cues – have a repertoire of clearly understood non-verbal cues

- Use of silence – when dealing with challenging students tactical pausing – naming the student and pausing for 5 seconds before giving a direction – is a powerful tool to use

CHAPTER 7

Managing anger and confrontation

This chapter looks at:

■ understanding why students and lecturers may become angry

■ analysing the physiology of anger

■ identifying the key stages of anger

■ 'how students express their anger' – strategies for lecturers to use with angry students

■ support and strategies we can give students

■ ways to reduce the chances of anger

We all have levels of adrenalin in our bodies; it was necessary for survival in the days when our ancestors lived in caves. In today's world we have few opportunites to make use of it and so we have to contrive situations in which it can be used. Hence the modern day phenomenon of 'rage'.

Examples of this include:

■ road rage

■ air rage

■ Tele-marketer rage

■ unsolicited calls rage

■ mobile phone rage

■ swimming pool lane rage

■ movie rage

■ sales rage

■ queue rage

■ supermarket trolley rage

Other occasions that can generate anger and rage are when people ignore you, challenge your competence, give unsolicited advice, don't appreciate you or when people are condescending towards you.

Understanding why students and lecturers become angry

Many students who misbehave are doing so to gain the attention of their peers and adults. Many of these students have very low self-esteem and have feelings of inadequacy. A number have inappropriate problem solving styles and are attempting to learn appropriate ways to behave.

According to Blum (2001), many students' aggressive displays in college are a form of play acting, 'testing out physical and mental boundaries through the rough and tumble of their interactions with each other and the teachers' (Blum, 2001: 7). This is especially apparent in students in college, who are at an age 'when egos are much more insecure and fragile than in fully fledged adults' (Blum, 2001: 7), and thus remarks can be misconstrued and result in aggressive behaviour. When adrenalin is released following a trigger situation, we spiral upwards into anger and aggression.

Everyone has some anger inside them; it is an explosive energy which is required for self-preservation. However, some students find themselves unable to cope with the demands of their situation and respond with anger. Sometimes transferring to a college can be traumatic – going to a large institution with older learners and a different curriculum can disrupt learners – even with the best induction programmes. Sometimes when students show anger towards lecturers they are using displacement. Often by our actions and social tone we may remind them of someone outside college who may be abusive towards them. Therefore inappropriate feelings are often displaced onto people and objects in college.

Many students do not have the emotional intelligence to decode the non-verbal and verbal communication that is occurring around them in order to understand when situations are likely to result in conflict. Also they do not have the vocabulary to negotiate and discuss situations. Remember that 'all behaviour is learnt'.

Students are good observers, but they don't always interpret situations well. Many potential conflicts could be avoided by effective communication:

'What makes me angry?'

'I make me angry.'

Analysing the physiology of anger

In order to develop strategies to successfully manage conflict situations in which anger arises it is important to understand the physiology of anger. According to Fisher (2005), the reptilian part of the brain is concerned with individual survival and developed whilst we were amphibians. It comes into action when we sense danger, increasing our heart rate, sending adrenalin surging through our body and gets us into a high state of alert and ready to respond with a fight, flight, freeze or flock response. Fisher also suggests this part of the brain can be 'stimulated by triggers related to deep-seated unresolved traumatic events in our life' (Fisher, 2005: 48) as cortisol released at the time of the earlier event suppresses the hippocampus which gives a context to the event. These strong emotional memories remain stored and can easily become a trigger for over-reaction in our own present lives. These emotional memories can impair our brain of the ability to think and reason effectively. Blood chemicals tell us to act and the message is so strong that our neo-cortex (the top part of the brain where we do most of our logical thinking and planning) cannot operate properly. An individual is flooded with feelings and cannot think properly.

Neural links between emotional and cognitive sites are greater in number than those from the cognitive to the emotional centres. It therefore takes longer for the thinking site to send back the information that the situation is not serious. Hence many people respond in an inappropriate manner because of the lag time involved. They are literally taken over by the emotion they are experiencing.

Think about our reaction to confrontational behaviour. When aroused, we tend to give an animal-like response: we become locked into a pattern of behaviour that sees increased states of arousal on both sides of the argument and irrationality takes over as the hormones kick in. How often have you observed someone in a conflict situation, when all rational thoughts seem to have disappeared. They are red faced, eyes bulging, and they are invading someone else's personal space.

Other types of unhelpful responses that might be triggered would include:

- Shouting
- Not listening to others views
- Bringing up past unrelated misdemeanours
- Standing toe to toe/face to face
- Raising our voices in response to theirs
- Allowing conflict to occur in a public forum
- Aggressive non-verbal communication – use of pointed fingers in the face
- Arms flailing
- Aggressive facial expressions (teeth showing)

Key stages of anger

It is important to understand the key stages of the anger process. The five stages are:

1 Trigger phase

2 Build-up phase

3 Crisis phase

4 Recovery phase (including possible additional outbursts)

5 Post-event depression

These five phases have been described by Long and Fogell (1999) as comprising an 'anger mountain'.

1 Trigger phase

Initially there is a trigger which signals a perceived danger or problem. The hormone adrenalin is then secreted.

2 Build-up phase

As we become more aroused we tend to lose the ability to think rationally. Our emotional arousal is energizing and makes us sharp and ready for action.

3 Crisis phase

This is when we reach the summit of our anger mountain. Now adrenalin is coursing through our veins and we reflect the hostile messages we may be getting. For example:

- Standing square on
- Inflating lungs so chest is bigger
- Making hostile eye contact
- Using arms as weapons

This is an extreme reaction but the excessively aggressive behaviour is seen as normal behaviour in abnormal circumstances.

4 Recovery phase

As the adrenalin surge drains away we move into the recovery phase. However, sometimes we may have additional possible outbursts when more adrenalin is secreted. This will lead to excessively aggressive behaviour again. When viewing CCTV footage of street crime, this is the phase when an aggressor returns to the victim he has just attacked and will carry out a further frenzied attack – in this additional outburst his anger knows no boundaries.

5 Post-event depression

After this surge of adrenalin most people feel very low and can suffer temporarily from post-event depression.

In the first three phases of anger we may display the following signs.

- Our face colour deepens
- We breathe faster
- There is an increase in perspiration
- We have dilated pupils

- We speak louder and faster

- We become agitated and fidgety and move faster

- We tense muscles, have a contorted face and clench our fists

- We have tightly closed lips

- We have hunched shoulders and a stiff rigid posture

- We are easily distracted and unfocused

- We use aggressive posturing and pointing fingers

Strategies for lecturers to use with angry students

- When faced with someone who is angry it is important to try to remain calm and acknowledge their feelings and point of view

- It is important not to take things personally

- Do not get hooked into a power struggle – keep responses low key

- Show respect towards the student; do not belittle or humiliate them

- Avoid having an emotional reaction to misbehaviour; put up a wall between yourself and what the student is doing

- Avoid becoming defensive

- Try to keep the situation in perspective

- Do not use dominant, threatening behaviour or show avoidance

- Avoid excessive eye contact as this can be seen as threatening and challenging. Allow the student to look away

- Avoid squaring up, invading their personal/intimate space (46cm) and any threatening movements. However, moving too far away might diminish your influence

- Do not try to mirror their mood. For example, if they shout and you then shout louder, this can lead to an upward spiral of confrontational behaviour. It is best to try to match the mood level, show some heightened response

- Convey non-aggressive intentions in your body language – avoid waving arms as this can exacerbate confrontation

- Use pauses between responses – a form of tactical pausing can reduce chances of adversarial confrontation

- Try to be solution-focused and allow the student to save face – give them an escape route

- Listen actively – respond to their feelings rather than their actions. Get them to talk it out. This avoids the chance of posturing

■ Show that you are willing to accept a compromise, a solution that is acceptable to all and allows everyone to feel a winner. Making token concessions can be good, admit that they may have a point (known as the 1 per cent technical error strategy)

■ Use inclusive language: people get angry so it's OK to feel that way and we will certainly be able to find a solution

■ Deferring the discipline and giving students time out to reflect can be a useful strategy, particularly if the student is not in the right mental state or conditions are not right. Buying a period of time for reflection is important

■ Avoid the 'oxygen of publicity' generated by public exchanges by taking the discussion somewhere private (but not away from a third party, otherwise you may be vulnerable)

■ Respect the right for people to disagree and have different opinions

■ Using attention diverters with distractions, real or imagined, can be a way of breaking the cycle of anger. For example – stand and look out of the window and say nothing – soon the student will join looking out of the window

■ Think about what you will do in certain situations – produce scripts for these

■ Sometimes you may need to use wrong-footing tactics and behave in a different way to what the student would normally expect from you

■ Try to establish a rapport by mirroring body language and listening to the language of their sensory preference (refer to Chapter 6)

■ Stay in control of yourself by checking your body language and speech volume. Keep clear of power struggles and avoid hostile remarks where sarcasm and ridicule are used

■ When in a conflict situation it is sometimes easy to make idle threats that can never be followed through. These must be avoided at all costs

■ Use humour to relieve the tension of the situation

■ Avoid the 'bad day' 'I am in a mood' syndrome that staff can have, given the pressures they face

Reflection on practice

List five ways in which we could create conflict as a lecturer when working with students.

1. _____

_____

2. _____

_____

3. _____

_____

4. _____

_____

5. _____

_____

Here are some suggestions to guide you. You might:

◆ Raise your voice

◆ Invade their personal space

◆ Use finger jabbing gestures

◆ Talk over them

◆ Not listen to them

◆ Refer to previous misdemeanours

◆ Deal with them in public and humiliate them

Now think of five ways in which you could diffuse conflict:

1. _____

_____

2. _____

_____

3. _____

_____

4. _____

_____

5. _____

_____

How students express their anger

How students express their anger in a conflict situation can have a lot to do with their anger styles. Although anger styles are learned they are deeply ingrained and are automatic, almost like reflexes.

Signs of a student becoming angry

In dealing with conflict it is helpful to be aware of some of the danger signals that denote conflict may be about to arise. The student may demonstrate the following behaviours:

- Unwilling to communicate

- Looking away when you speak

- Pacing around, unwilling to remain in seat

- Outbursts of temper

- Frequent repeating of certain phrases

- False, sarcastic laughter

- Sweating

- Shortness of breath or rapid breathing

- Unable to settle to work

- Appears agitated

- Easily distracted

- Eyes bulging/pupils dilated

- Stiff, rigid posture

- Rapid body movements

'Acting in' and 'Acting out'

Based upon work by Schmidt (1993), Long and Fogell (1999) suggested that students express their anger and challenge by 'acting in' or 'acting out'. The categories they presented are discussed below.

Acting in

Students who 'act in' attack themselves with self-damaging behaviour. They appear anxious, depressed, withdrawn, passive and unmotivated. There is an apparent irrational refusal to respond and cooperate. Two types of 'acting in' roles are:

- **Stuffers**

  - Hold in anger and deny they are angry

  - Avoid confrontation at all costs

  - Suffer from depression and illnesses

- **Withdrawers**

  - Express their anger by withdrawing from others

  - By doing this they protect themselves from the cause of the anger whilst also punishing those who caused it

When working with Stuffers and Withdrawers:

- Mirror how they act and model appropriate strategies they could use to help themselves

- Get them to use positive affirmations – positive statements to raise self-esteem at problem times

- Get them to log incidents where they withdrew or held their anger; give them alternative approaches for the next occasion

- Use drama therapy to help them; use of story is also a powerful tool in emotional literacy

Acting out

Students who 'act out' tend to be aggressive, threatening, demanding of attention, disruptive and will prevent others from working. Two types of acting out roles are:

- **Blamers**

  ❏ Have little belief that they can make things better for themselves

  ❏ Blame others for their angry feelings

  ❏ Can tease and name call

- **Exploders**

  ❏ Express their anger through direct and immediate confrontation

  ❏ Have short fuses and are physically or verbally aggressive towards peers and adults

When working with Blamers and Exploders:

- Provide regular contact with a mentor or behavioural assistant

- Use a positive restitution approach, where the aggressor has to meet and make it up with the victim

- Focus the reprimand on the behaviour not the student

- Use behaviour modification strategies to recognize and praise them when they get it right

Fisher (2005), quoting work by Lee (1993), identified four anger styles that individuals display. Fisher also added his own fifth style, 'the Winder-Upper'. These styles are:

- **The Intimidator:** Controls others through an aggressive standpoint

- **The Interrogator:** Controls others through manipulation – through finding fault, and making people feel self-conscious and guilty

- **Poor Me:** Makes people feel guilty by them not doing enough for me

- **Distancer:** Seeks to control others by remaining detached, unapproachable and vague

- **The Winder-Upper:** Seeks to control through humour – joking, teasing or mocking others

Students tend to get stuck in a particular way of managing their behaviour. In supporting students to manage their anger and confrontation effectively we need to get them to understand the physical signs in themselves and others when they are about to lose their temper. We need to:

- Give them specific intervention strategies to use to reduce their feelings of anger

- Develop relaxation/stress reduction techniques that they can use

Support and strategies we can give students

Some examples of the support we can give are:

- **Dramatherapy:** Through music and drama we can help students to understand how to identify signs of anger and how to control their feelings. We can also give them an active vocabulary to use to negotiate in such situations

- **Mirroring and modelling:** Gaining students' permission to mirror their non-verbal and verbal communication when they are getting angry might be a useful strategy. If you mirror some of the signs this will increase their awareness of when they are getting angry. Then model some strategies that they may use to reduce their feeling of anger: such as breathing exercises, counting to ten, progressive muscle tensing and relaxation

- **'Fire drills':** Give students strategies to use in conflict situations. Get them to rehearse what to do, particularly how they should react to an angry student in the classroom

- **Developing positive self-talk:** Get students to list four or five statements that they can think of when faced with another person's anger. This will help them to diffuse chances of conflict:

  ❑ I am not responsible for this person's feelings

  ❑ People say things they don't mean when they are angry

  ❑ Who makes me angry? I am the only person who can make me angry

  ❑ I can reduce the tension by remaining calm

- **Giving students strategies to reduce stress**

  ❑ Relaxation techniques – visualization

  ❑ Tension releasers – beanbags/stress balls

- **Changing negative feelings:** Help students to reframe negative feelings. Many angry students have very low levels of self-esteem and have fragile egos. If someone pushes them or knocks into them in the corridor they believe that they wanted to hurt them or start a fight. We need to develop more neutral thoughts in students: perhaps the person lost their balance or they were not looking where they were going. This is a long term process that will ultimatley help students

- **Reflecting on causes of conflict:** Get students to reflect on causes of anger. What triggers them into anger and conflict? Get them to keep an Anger Diary and record incidents of anger and their triggers. Work through this with them and develop strategies that students could use in response to the triggers

- **Developing 'I' statements** to rationalize their behaviour and to give them a script to use with the other person in the conflict. For example – 'When you do [x] (behaviour), I feel upset (feeling) because I cannot do my work (effect). I would like to [x] (proposed solution)'

- **Reframing:** Students who behave badly tend to have extremely low self-esteem and a very negative self-image; they think that 'everyone in the world has it in for me'. This self-downing has been described as 'psychological junk mail'. It affects students' ability to cope. There is a need to reframe the problem, looking at it realistically and to get students to reframe the negatives into positives. It has been described as 'looking for the good in every situation'

- **Goal setting and practice of skills:** 'One small step' and 'a day at a time' would be key phrases to use. Setting easy-to-achieve targets and allowing opportunities to practise new patterns of behaviour in small steps would be good as this ensures success. Front-loaded reward systems are also important so that students are initially rewarded frequently for modification of their behaviour

- **Time Out Card:** When students are finding it difficult to cope in sessions they can be issued with a 'Time Out Card' for a limited period. The aim of the card is to enable them to leave a lesson when conditions are such that may do something they will regret. For example, another student is winding them up so much that they may retaliate or the lecturer may say something that may cause the student to explode. When a student feels that they may have to leave a lesson, because their anger may explode, they show the card to their lecturer who lets them leave the room to cool off. On leaving the session the student is expected to find a nominated member of staff who will spend time with them discussing the causes of their problem at that time and will give them strategies to cope. The card is signed by the member of staff to show arrival and departure time. In the 10 years that I have used this system the students, lecturers and myself have found it a most useful way to reduce conflict. It has not been abused and students value and appreciate the time to reflect and have some space

- Peer mediation: Involving a neutral third party to mediate and help settle conflict and disputes between students has been very successful in a number of institutions. This is a voluntary role and is not about making judgements as to who is right or wrong. The aim of the mediator is to help disputants resolve their conflict. Skills needed by the mediators are:

❏ good speaking and listening skills

❏ the ability to heed the views, needs and feelings of disputants

❏ the ability to find solutions – resolution skills

Peer mediation develops students' problem solving ability and works because it empowers students to attempt to resolve conflict. It helps to develop a positive ethos where there is trust and open communication. There are also positive relationships. Former troublesome students have been found to be very effective mediators: 'poacher turned gamekeeper'. They have first hand experience of disputes and enjoy taking on the responsibility of settling disputes through negotiation.

■ **Circle time**: When students experience problems in relationships with other students or staff resentments and anger may build over a period of time which, if not dealt with, can lead to serious repercussions for the student and others with whom he or she may come into contact. One technique that is used in many institutions to try to deal with such potential conflict is circle time, when students sit in a circle and discuss their problems and successes. Clear protocols/rules are established for the group. For example:

❏ Everyone has the right to express their feelings without being put down

❏ Only one person may speak at any time. Sharing experiences and feelings openly is accepted by all group members

❏ A positive atmosphere has to be maintained

❏ The group leader thanks each member for their contributions

Group members are encouraged to be supportive and 'the circle' offers advice on how students should react in the future. Where circle time is operated it has a most beneficial effect on behaviour and helping students to find solutions. I have seen this work well in tutor sessions with students.

Approaches to reduce chances of conflict

■ Attempt to anticipate inappropriate behaviour by looking for signs and triggers in the student and in yourself

■ Have a calm, non-confrontational approach when facing confrontational behaviour from a student

■ Respond rather than react. When responding make sure you do so constructively

■ Listen to what the student has to say

■ Do not allow the situation to escalate

■ Defuse your own instinctive reactions by using established routines

- Permit the student some dignity

- Do not invade their personal space

- Use gestures and phrases you have rehearsed and successfully used previously

- Use friendly gestures. Do not point. Use the palms of your hands or place your hands by your side

- Stand sideways on. Do not face the individual. This stance is less threatening

- Do not mirror their mood. If you become equally angry, or remain calm, this can escalate confrontation. Reflect an increase in emotional level to show that you are really concerned

- Always explain to students the reasons for your actions

- Try to get the other person to think positively about the situation. Get them to reframe negative thoughts and give them a positive spin

- Show genuine concern and help the student to take control of the situation

- Make a token concession – 'Well I have to admit it could have been dealt with better!'

- If necessary give time and space for both of you to calm down

- Do not back a student into a corner, demanding an immediate response

- Allow the student to save face – the older the student the more important it is for them to have a way out

- Treat each case individually. It may be necessary to treat people differently, using different strategies from our repertoire

- Use appropriate humour, to lighten the situation. In my research students have stated that appropriate humour can reduce conflict

- Attempt to divert the student by using distracting techniques – 'Did you just see that strange animal walk past outside?'

- At the same time, however, show that you are taking the student seriously

- When a student is intent on disruption and conflict, thank them for their comments and ask them to discuss it with you at the end of the lesson – this helps to keep them guessing

- Remove the student from the oxygen of publicity – the situation is likely to get worse if acted out in front of their peers

- Remember that silence can be very effective

- When reading non-verbal communication in students we can easily become misled. Do not read single examples of non-verbal communication – always read 'gesture clusters'. Look for congruence between non-verbal and verbal forms of communication

- When students misbehave it is important to refer to their rights and responsibilities – they are infringing the rights of others and in doing so are not fulfilling their responsibilities. Supporting students by giving them an understanding of their rights and responsibilities and the skills necessary to fulfil them is important

- Wrong-footing the student by responding in an unpredictable manner can help de-escalate the situation and reduce the chances of the conflict getting out of control

- Gaining students' permission to mirror their non-verbal and verbal language when they are getting angry can be a useful strategy as it will increase their awareness of when they are beginning to lose control. Model some strategies that they may use to reduce their feeling of anger, such as breathing exercises

In conclusion, it is important when faced with conflict not to get sucked into an upward spiral. Some groups of students frequently try to take control in the learning environment by testing us. By being calm, assertive, aware, firm and consistent we will be able to keep in control. When the going gets tough remember not to take the things angry students say personally as an angry child knows no boundaries and often young people are testing what is acceptable behaviour in the safest environment they know, the college.

Key points to remember

- The reptilian part of the brain is concerned with survival and when triggered it senses danger and sends adrenalin surging through our veins. We are then in a high state of alert and are ready to respond with a fight, flight, freeze or flock response

- This part of the brain can be triggered by deep-seated unresolved traumatic events in our lives

- Students do not have the emotional intelligence to decode the non-verbal and verbal communication used towards them to understand when situations are likely to result in conflict. Neither do they have the skills to negotiate their way out of these situations

- There are five stages to anger:

  ❑ Trigger phase

  ❑ Build-up phase

  ❑ Crisis phase

  ❑ Recovery phase (including possible additional outbursts)

  ❑ Post-event depression

- There are clear physical signs that someone is about to become angry

- There are five anger styles. These are:

  ❑ The Intimidator

  ❑ The Interrogator

- ❑ Poor Me

- ❑ The Distancer

- ❑ The Winder-Upper

■ Students 'act in' or 'act out' anger

■ Support and strategies we can give students include:

- ❑ Drama therapy

- ❑ Mirroring and modelling

- ❑ 'Fire drills'

- ❑ Developing positive self-talk

- ❑ Giving students strategies to reduce stress

- ❑ Reframing – removing negative self-talk – 'the psychological junk mail'

- ❑ Goal setting

- ❑ Time Out Card

- ❑ Peer mediation

Managing difficult groups

This chapter looks at:

■ use of a Neuro-Linguistic Programming approach to manage challenging groups of learners

■ getting alpha males and females onside

■ managing badly behaving boys

■ strategies to use with difficult groups

■ understanding the roles students may play in challenging groups

■ groups that interact poorly with one another

■ support strategies and rewards for managing difficult groups

■ use of cooperative learning strategies to develop difficult groups

■ stimulating activities to engage challenging learners

■ managing difficult groups in practical and workshop areas

Classroom events can be simultaneous, and with a difficult class, this can be seen as overwhelming … There is a manic fairground game whereby crocodiles pop their heads up at unpredictable locations and time intervals – the object of the game is to smack the heads down with a mallet as fast as possible before the next one pops up. Teaching any class with a large disruptive element feels much like this game – minus the mallets …! (Mathieson and Price, 2002: 56)

We have all faced classes that are particularly challenging. It sometimes appears as though all the worst-behaved students have been put together in the same class. At the end of sessions with these groups we have to reach for the headache tablets or feel as though we need a stiff drink. Chris Watkins (1999) suggested that managing such groups in the classroom is 'perhaps the most complex and least understood situation on the planet'. Managing badly behaving groups in the classroom is a bit like air traffic control: dealing with students in these situations tends to be like trying to land 10 jumbo jets on the same piece of runway at the same time. It is the unpredictability and simultaneity of events that makes our job so challenging. Mathieson and Price (2002: 56) suggest that in managing behaviour in the classroom 'we are highly visible to all the other participants … which brings its own vulnerability'.

The groups of students you meet as part of the Increased Flexibility Programme will come from a number of different schools. A number of these students will have been selected to go on this programme because they display extremely challenging behaviour and are likely to be on the verge of exclusion. Put a number of these characters together and the first few sessions will be about them trying to gain the top position in the group. This will involve physical and verbal aggression and can make it almost impossible to do your job. To be successful you will need to develop a number of team building exercises to help gel the group.

Using a neuro-linguistic programming approach to managing challenging groups of learners

The identification of ring leaders will be essential. To demonstrate the power of body language in managing behaviour let us look at **strategy elicitation**. This is where a member of staff picks out the leader in a group early in each lesson and engages them in eye contact and using other non-verbal interactors. Elicitation is the technique for assisting someone else to move from one state to another. Through Neuro-Linguistic Programming (NLP) researchers have tried to identify the strategies used by teachers who are successful in managing behaviour. Berry (2003) discussed how research has attempted to identify the internal and external actions of successful staff and have tried to get other staff to replicate the same actions. Berry (2003) suggested that successful staff are very aware of the power of non-verbal communication. When settling groups they will identify a group of four or five influencers and leaders in the class and engage them in eye contact, giving non-verbal cues that they want them to settle. These cues are also effective in controlling poor behaviour. The sequence in which the member of staff looks at the group of four or five is critical, as is the duration of the stare and the lecturer's position in the room. The sequence of non-verbal cues is important. Anyone observing this opening must replicate the sequence accurately. Any changes in sequence, duration or type of non-verbal signals and they will not have the same level of success.

Getting alpha males and females onside

It is important that we identify the leaders in our groups – the 'alpha' males and females. The terms come from the study of animal behaviour, which have shown that there is normally a dominant member of the pack. The term 'alpha male' was first used to describe aggressive American politicians in the 1950s.

Typical alpha males will have a dress code that identifies them as belonging to a group or gang – hoodies, baseball caps or bandanas – but they are likely to be physically bigger than their peers and will be of above-average intelligence (see further Vizard, 2003).

A parallel you may have seen in the animal kingdom would be the baboon that sits at the top of the baboon rock at the local zoo.

Once you have identified them, you need to work to get these males onside. For example one group of alpha males I met made disparaging comments to other students who were presented with awards in assembly, so I devised a strategy to undermine their actions. I gave rewards to them for every small action – so that they were the ones coming to the front in the gathering. This soon stopped their calling out. I then identified something that they wanted as a group – a Social Area. I got the necessary funding and we worked together to build it in our free time. This time was used for some higher-grade male bonding. For some students, however, a stronger line has to be taken – a coercive approach, based on a testosterone fuelled battle of wills.

It was once thought that boys were the key students to target in behaviour management schemes. However, alpha females and girls displaying ladette behaviour are becoming loud, assertive and every bit as disruptive in lessons. Jackson (2006) conducted a survey of 1,000 students in schools in the North of England and found that there has been an increase in ladette behaviour, with a growing number of teenage girls being rowdy, swearing and fighting.

Alpha females tend to show their traits from the age of 7 or 8. They tend to be sharper and brighter than their peers. They are as competitive as men and their bullying is subtle and cruel (see further Wyatt, 2002). Besag (2006) has suggested that girls are more effective bullies than boys and use psychological warfare to dominate their victims. Alpha females use psychological techniques to bully other girls. Girls rarely use violence but use a subtle undermining of confidence of others, which can be far more damaging and have lifelong effects on some victims. Some nasty tricks used include:

- Making a girl drop her old friends if she wants to join the in-group, then exclude her anyway

- Missing the victim out of a party invitation or encouraging a victim to organize a party then ensuring no one turns up

- Stealing a victim's workbook from the homework pile and hiding it

- Starting rumours about the victim

Friendship appears more important to girls than academic success. They fear isolation after being pushed out of a friendship group. According to information presented to a House of Commons Education Select Committee, girls use 'rumour-mongering and "social isolation"' to control their victims. David Moore (2006), a Senior Ofsted Inspector highlighted the use of non-verbal communication as a powerful weapon. For example, a group of girls would walk up to another girl who thinks they are all friends and then walk away, isolating her and leaving her publicly humiliated. Girls typically exclude others from their circle by cruel words and devious back-stabbing. They can be obsessed by the consumer culture, with its emphasis on clothes and looks. They are supremely confident.

An alpha female's position needs to be undermined by removing members of her gang in the class and engaging her in activities working with other groups of students. It is important to ensure that the students she has isolated feel secure and involved in the class; lecturers need to give them more of their time.

Some alpha males and females may also require support and counselling to help them understand why they have assumed this role. They can be given strategies to help them follow alternative routes.

Managing badly behaving boys

When facing challenging behaviour by groups of students, we find these groups are most likely to be made up of boys. Boys are four times more likely than girls to be excluded; 83 per cent of all secondary exclusions involve boys (Osler et al., 2002).

Male students in this age group 'hunt in packs' and to them peer group influences are very important. They can work together in class and have a very destructive effect. Boys enjoy the 'instant gratification' they get from the response of lecturers and fellow students when they misbehave. Many students are 'eager to please', but this is not the case with this group.

The following strategies can help reduce the effect of this group.

- Have male and female students in mixed seating arrangements

- Males enjoy sociable learning, but get them to work in groups/pairs other than their friendship groups

- Engage male students in active learning. Time-limited tasks should be used, where they have to transform learning from one medium to another (for example, video/play to oral report). In many classrooms the male students are expected to learn passively

- Introduce a trial and error speculative approach to learning – this is an experimental approach in which learners understand that it is OK to make mistakes

- Be aware that males have a low boredom threshold and shorter attention span – plan a larger number of shorter tasks

- A clear structure is needed for their work. Have protocols established for various activities

- Males may only be able to do one thing at a time – remember this fact when planning activities

- Remember that among males it is not seen as being 'cool' to learn. Males do not like to stand out and so underachieve. They also like to gain notoriety through poor behaviour. Institutions often perpetuate this situation by continuing to tolerate the 'anti-boffin culture'

Strategies to use with difficult groups

When faced with poor behaviours in a challenging group we need to become Miss Marple or Hercule Poirot and try to play the detective. Ask why is this behaviour being done with me in this setting? Look at the antecedents to the behaviour. Try to identify the triggers to the behaviour. Then identify how the behaviour manifested itself. Also try to identify the consequence or pay-off for the student. If we reflect on poor behaviour in this way we develop successful strategies to manage the behaviour. Learning Support staff may easily be able to identify all of the above. They may also be able to identify a solution-focused approach for a particular student and explain where the poor behaviour is least likely to occur and what strategies are used by that member of staff.

More general strategies we can use include the following.

- Many students are testing boundaries to see how far they may be able to go. To stay in control you need to give all learners a structure, a routine and firm boundaries

- You should have a flexibility in your repertoire and should be able to make a sudden change in your manner when necessary

- It is important to make it difficult for students to read you – a little unpredictability is important

- Early intervention is essential, by predicting what poor behaviours are likely to occur before they ever start

- It is important to have blitzes on particular areas of poor behaviour throughout the year

Do not take poor behaviour as a personal attack. This is very unlikely and the student is most often experimenting to learn how to behave appropriately by testing the boundaries in a safe environment. Also, some students have bad behaviour so deeply ingrained in them, very often as a survival strategy in their lives outside college, that they are not even aware of the fact they are behaving badly. Think of how we drive a car. Our driving skills are so deeply ingrained that we do not think about what we are doing at a conscious level. Something similar may be happening with your students who are demonstrating challenging behaviour.

Many students can give the appearance of being supremely confident while in fact they have low self-esteem and struggle to gain the recognition of their peers. Many can become involved in poor behaviour with others to gain plaudits from the peer group. Michael Marland (2001) suggested that these students 'get caught up in what is called "the prison of the peer groups" – they pretend they are toughly being themselves when actually they have been cast in the role of trouble makers and are happy with the casting and are seeking the satisfaction of others, admiring their troublesome role'.

With that in mind, let us now consider some of the roles students may play in a group.

Understanding the roles students may play in challenging groups

The key to successful behaviour management of difficult groups is to identify the student roles within the group and use this to your advantage.

Key roles of students

- **Alpha male:** Above-average intelligence, usually physically bigger

- **Alpha female:** Above-average intelligence, dressed in latest fashions, uses sarcasm to control

- **Instigator:** Starts trouble but usually gets away with it by being surreptitious

- **Regulator/Questioner:** Constantly interrupts, asking the same question in many different ways; these students are very disruptive

- **Deflector/Attention Diverter:** Takes the heat off a student in trouble by deflecting the lecturer's attention by smart comments or minor misbehaviour

- **Disruptor:** Tactically aware – intervenes with the intention of disrupting when a lecturer is trying to regain control of a group

- **Orchestrator:** Coordinates much of the bad behaviour, acting as a conductor to the symphony of bad behaviour, orchestrating outbursts from group to group

- **Class Clown/Joker:** The class entertainer, who can be difficult to manage. However, when there is a tense moment they can defuse it by making an amusing comment. Sometimes they take on this role because they have a poor self-image and feel inadequate. They make fun of themselves before someone else does

- **Fall Guys/Professional Victim:** Male or female student who is happy to take the wrap for things

- **Challengers:** Enjoys challenging the rules and instructions given to them. Such students often grandstand by making a late entrance – to gain the plaudits of their peer group

- **Invisible Person:** Sometimes known as the 'radiator kid' – clinging to the radiator afraid to move away from this zone of security. This student may be a victim of bullying or may be suffering 'post-traumatic stress disorder'

- **Manipulator:** Attempts to manipulate students around them to do their work or gets them into trouble with staff. Such students get a feeling of self-satisfaction when they are successful

- **Covert Operator:** Appears pleasant but under the surface is undermining the lecturer's authority. These students do not do what is asked of them, but this would not be obvious to an observer

- **Constant Rule Breaker:** Challenges rules and tests boundaries. When told not to step over a line their toes inevitably drift towards and just over it

- **Know-All:** Thinks they know everything. They have covered each topic in more detail previously or will just say they have and will challenge decisions and query tasks set. Theses students can be extremely oppositional

- **Attention Seeker:** Wants to be centre stage and under the spotlight at all times. Such students will do whatever is necessary to be the centre of attention

- **Flirts:** Flirts with staff and other students to get attention and help

- **Passive students:** Fear failure, rejection and relationships. They keep their heads down.

- **Sheep/Followers:** Those student who blindly follow what others do

- **Aggressive/hostile students:** Those who act out their feelings in an aggressive manner. They are hostile to their peers and staff. They may often be bullies

- **Antagonistic students:** Constantly niggle and annoy everyone around them

- **Fog Horns/Shouters:** Students who talk loudly and with excessive volume for the environment they are in to gain the positive or negative attention of others

Reflection on practice

1 Identify a class of students who offer high levels of challenging behaviour

2 Try to ascribe the roles described above that key members play

3 Are there any additional roles that you could add to the list?

4 Identify some strategies that may work to help to develop a good working atmosphere

5 What whole class reward systems could be developed to develop good relationships?

6 Describe how the rewards system could be developed to make a more positive working environment

7 Think how this could be done:

Tangibly

Verbally

Non-verbally

Groups that interact poorly with one another

Poor interpersonal relationships between students in a particular class may often lead to discipline problems for lecturers. Endless disputes amongst the students can make the group very difficult to teach and can have a debilitating effect on the lecturer.

With such groups the following strategies may be useful:

- Hold meetings of staff who normally teach the group

- Identify types of poor behaviour and *how* the group is dysfunctional

- Select five examples of poor behaviour and reach agreement on three ways you will deal with each behaviour

- Consistency is the key: if students experience a consistent approach, then there will be a reduction in poor behaviour. (You could employ the consistency model exercise used in Chapter 9)

- Develop a rewards system. Identify the types of poor behaviour you would like to reduce. For example, in dealing with a group in which students are making inappropriate comments to one another:

  ❏ Inform students that you will be keeping a tally of negative and positive comments during the lesson

  ❏ Set targets that you want them to achieve in relation to the ratio of positive to negative comments

  ❏ Also give them examples of positive comments that can be made to each other

❏ If targets are achieved issue a reward for the group

❏ If any students attempt to sabotage the system have a punishment system in place – for example, isolation/withdrawal

Sometimes it may be necessary to develop a series of activities to encourage greater cooperation and aid socialization amongst group members. These activities could improve positivity and cohesion amongst classes. The activities would be of a team building nature, with some offering a high level of challenge. A number of these activities would be needed to cover a wide variety of personal skills. The emphasis would be on:

■ total group involvement

■ constructive communication

■ positive cooperation

■ good discipline and behaviour

■ sensible use of personal skills within groups

■ punctuality

Lecturers, when faced with groups such as these, tend to become very negative, they generalize and say that they are out of control, when they are not. With such groups there will be times that are less bad. Remember them. Always attempt to anticipate the bad behaviour. When groups are badly behaved, use it as a learning experience. Sometimes changing the way you organize a group for activities can improve the behaviour.

Developing cooperative learning strategies can be good. You could divide students into groups of five where each group member has a specific role. All group members would have to work cooperatively for the task to be achieved. Using cooperative learning leads to better behaviour and the development of interpersonal skills.

Support strategies and rewards for managing difficult groups

Some support strategies that could be used with difficult groups are:

■ Attaching students to a Mentor or 'Charismatic Hero'. Some colleges attach senior staff to these students to guide them

■ Having line managers drop in on a lesson involving badly behaving groups and maintaining a high profile in lesson time

■ Using adults external to the college as mentors. This could involve using inter-generational schemes, people from business, sportsmen and women, engineers, or people from the world of music, including DJs

■ Engaging disaffected students in a student-run radio station, writing a daily news sheet including news, quizzes and music pages to be used by all students at registration

- Increasing motivation through schemes linking sporting successes with achievement in the classroom

- Involving students in contemporary drama, which engages students in discussing key issues and allows them a safe framework for experimenting with concepts and ideas

- Giving these students a whole range of responsibilities

Some other strategies that could be used include:

- Put names in a pot and have a raffle to select seats

- Split troublesome groups and use these students as leaders

- Use those students as helpers and monitors

- In groups, give rewards to a group if they are successful at a task. Misbehaviour by any member of the group results in no reward

- Stealth tactics – introduce individual tasks that divert them – so that they don't realize they have been split

- Ensure they have work that they can cope with, be successful with and of which they can be proud

- Have short, structured activities that allow for instant gratification

- Establish ground rules – group ownership and responsibility

- Have differentiated activities – with competitions and rewards

- Identify roles played by group members and try to use strategies to disempower them

- Try to develop a positive group identity

Using cooperative learning strategies to develop difficult groups

Tell me
I'll forget

Show me
I may remember

But involve me
and I will
understand
　(Chinese Proverb)

Many students displaying challenging behaviour are likely to be kinaesthetic learners. This is why 14–16 year old learners really enjoy their experiences in Further Education, which offers them an outlet for their kinaesthetic energy in the variety of practical subjects they experience. So certainly, 'involve me and I will understand' is a reason for their success in college.

How we organize and structure the learning experiences can be important – particularly in the theory and portfolio sessions. Cooperative learning strategies can be a good approach, requiring students to cooperate with each other as they learn. The lesson is structured so that students have a vested interest in each other's learning as well as their own. This approach can be very challenging to students but it is highly effective academically and socially.

Jigsaw techniques

The jigsaw technique is one approach to developing cooperative learning. Students are divided into groups of five and each group discusses five aspects of a particular topic. A Catering Lecturer in one college has used this approach to get students to think about ways of cooking five different meats – such as turkey, chicken, beef, lamb and pork. One member of each group is responsible for the approach to cooking one of the categories of meat. After a short period students re-group into groups relating to the meat they discussed – for example, all the beefs together. They then become a specialist group and come up with the best three ways to cook their meat. Each group then prepares a report to give to the other groups. A variation on this would be to have each group specializing on ways to cook one meat. Then students are re-grouped so that one member from the beef group joins one member from the lamb, pork, turkey and chicken groups. Each person has to present the ways decided to cook their meat to the rest of the group.

Another way to use this approach is to set up five resource areas in the room to do with a topic. For example, Internet access, posters, book resources, audio/video/DVD and an expert. Students in groups of five allocate one student in each group to visit one area. They then return having collected key information to feed back to other members of their group.

There are many strengths to this approach and they include:

- High levels of challenge

- Greater involvement of group members

- It is empowering

- It involves peer teaching

- It is task based/learning by doing

- It involves active learning

- Motivation is raised

- Social skills are developed

- There is a higher level of reasoning

Stimulating activities to engage challenging learners

With the current emphasis on personalized learning, it is important to understand the style diversity of learners so that we can develop a range of activities that will match their individual learning profiles. Each learner will have a unique profile. Barbara Prashnig (2006) developed Learning Style Analysis for Learners, whereby learners complete questionnaires that look at issues such as hemispheric dominance, sensory preference, brain processing, thinking style, environments in which they work best – relating to light, sound and temperature – and social group preference from alone to team working. Another part of this profile could include Howard Gardner's Multiple Intelligences (Gardner and Hatch, 1989) where every individual has a balance of intelligences – these include interpersonal, intrapersonal, linguistic, mathematic and logical, visual and spatial, kinaesthetic, musical and naturalist. Using the Learning Style Analysis, an individual and group profile can be produced.

The best way to motivate learners and help them learn information is to get them actively involved. The most effective way to achieve retention of learning is to have young people practise by doing, and where they teach others and make immediate use of their learning. Using these two approaches will give 75 per cent and 90 per cent average retention rates respectively, according to George (1995). Having a range of starter activities at the beginning of the session can be a way of focusing learners early or be used as a brain break to break up work in the session. A sample of some activities that can be used is given below:

Jigsaw pieces

- Cut up 10 postcards of various images to do with the subject matter into at least 10 pieces and jumble up the pieces into 10 envelopes

- Divide students into groups of three and each group is given an envelope with the jumbled pieces and a picture of the card they are to make

- Students then have to assemble the picture by negotiating swaps with other learners

- For example, I have successfully used a Jigsaw World Atlas, which has six jigsaws of six continents (see Voakes and King, 2004)

Clock Patience

- Write key information on 12 postcards. For example, Kitchen French – with the English word on one side and the French term on the back of the card

- Students place cards out as a clock face with the English term uppermost

- Students then pick up the card at the 12 o'clock position, read the English phrase and then look at the French phrase and say it. They move to 1 o'clock and do the same before returning to 12 o'clock and here they say the English word and then French phrase without lifting the card and do the same at 1 o'clock before moving on to 2 o'clock. The whole process is repeated until student has worked around the 'clock face'. Some phrases will be repeated up to 12 times

Splat

■ List 20 key words on the whiteboard, get two students to stand at the front with fly swats. The group gives a clue to the word, and the first student to splat that word gets a point. Work until the first student has five splats

Tearing Off a Strip

■ Write 21 key words on the board. Students have to list eight of them on a strip of paper, divided into eight boxes

■ You call out words randomly and if the word is at the top or bottom of the student's paper, they tear it off

■ This process continues until a student has torn off all the words on their list. First one to do so is the winner

■ Then put the students into pairs and they take turns, with the other student's permission, to doodle the word on the back of their partner with their finger. When the word is identified by their partner they swap roles. This process goes on until all 16 words have been identified. The first students to be seated are winners

All of a Jumble

■ Read out key words to do with your subject but with the letters jumbled up. Get students to identify the terms. For example, with Building and Construction:

❑ STRANGE LIP = PLASTERING

❑ CENT ME = CEMENT

❑ NUTS IN A FOOD = FOUNDATIONS

❑ BUNG LIMP = PLUMBING

❑ NICE ARTICLE = ELECTRICIAN

❑ I WRING = WIRING

Battleships

■ The game is played the traditional way in pairs, but to have a go students have to have answered a question related to their subject correctly, posed by their partner

■ Lecturers can issue different prepared question sheets

■ Another variation is to make the battleships up out of a number of words to do with the subject

■ One five letter word, three four letter words and so on. When a hit is scored, students have to give the letter and the size of the word

Feely Bag

- There are five items in the bag which relate to the day's lesson

- One person puts their hand in the bag and describes what they feel. The others discuss what it might be and how it relates to the topic

Twenty-Four

- Give students a list of 24 words, in sets of four words with three words linked and the additional one as an odd one out, but still related to the topic (the example given below relates to Hair and Beauty)

- Get them to spot the odd one out from each set of four words and say why it is the odd one out. For example: gel, conditioner, brush, shampoo. Brush is the odd one out as the other three are a liquid hair product

- Get students to add another word to each set of four words which links to the three that are related and still leaves the additional word the odd one out. For example: gel, conditioner, brush, shampoo, spray. Brush is still the odd one out

- Then get students to make up their own lists of four words as above

An excellent range of starter activities can be found at http://atschool.eduweb.co.uk/ ufa10/starters/. These are particularly useful in numeracy sessions but could be used in a variety of other subjects. A starter is produced for each day of the year and they relate to the season/festival. Another site rich in ideas for starter activities is www.quizardry.com.

Getting students to stand is energizing and will put 15 per cent more oxygen in their brains. If you introduce brain break activities which link the left and right brain by the coordinated movement between left and right arms and legs, this will improve students' ability to learn.

Alphabet Brain Gym (listening activity)

- Have the alphabet written around the room with letters L, R or T under each letter

- You then say a word to do with your subject and read it a letter at a time

- Students then have to look at the chart and move their arms or/and legs according to the letter next to the alphabet letter:

    L = Left hand or/and leg

    R = Right hand or/and leg

    T = Place left or right hand or/and leg together

Double Doodles

- Students doodle in the air with their arms and spell out the same words to do with the subject simultaneously with left and right hands. Lots of very interesting activities are listed at www.braingym.org (see also Ballinger, 1996)

Sitting and running on the spot/Swimming on the spot

- Doing different strokes and leg movements with each hand/foot whilst seated

Managing difficult groups in practical and workshop areas

Case Study: Building and Construction practical areas

In one college a lecturer had organized his workshop in a particularly successful way. During the day he had two IFP groups from two schools arriving at staggered times. The first group arrived at 9am, the next at 10am. There was a clear routine for each group to follow. On arrival they assembled in a small classroom area attached to the practical area. Here the students chatted with the lecturer as tasks for the session were allocated. Relationships were excellent and the lecturer even gave up time to referee the students in a football match at lunchtime. Students then went to put on their protective clothing, boots and goggles. Each group were experiencing tiling, plastering and bricklaying and some elementary carpentry on a rotating programme. So in the room at any one time there were groups of students involved in four activities. When the second group arrived the same routine was followed. It was also interesting to note that these students then integrated well with peers from other schools in the same workshop area. At the end of the session following clearing up and changing, students gathered in the classroom area for a debrief and for planning for next the session.

This session, with difficult and challenging students, worked well because of the structure, organisation and routine established by the lecturer. A lot also depended on the good relationship set up by the lecturer during the establishment phase.

Key points to remember

- Have an inbuilt flexibility in your repertoire

- Early intervention is essential

- Play the detective – why is a group or an individual being difficult? Look for triggers and pay off

- Identify roles being played by group members

- Identify alpha males and females and use strategy elicitation

- Understand the traits of the macho culture in some learning environments

- Use a range of strategies, including those in this chapter

- With groups that do not relate well to one another, use behaviour modification strategies – set small-scale targets for improvement and reward when achieved

- Use group building activities regularly

- Regularly use cooperative learning strategies

- Use the range of starter activities and brain break strategies outlined

CHAPTER 9

Establishing a consistent approach

This chapter will look at:

- adopting a consistent approach in the way we manage behaviour

- how to develop a Consistency Model amongst staff teams

- strategies to manage effectively a range of typical challenging behaviours

Students in college, particularly those in the 14–16 age group, need to be managed in a consistent manner. Most students enjoy working in environments where firm, clear and predictable boundaries are set.

If you track an individual student during a day you will see that they are dealt with in different ways from lecturer to lecturer. There is a lack of consistency in how a student is dealt with in each session. Different Health and Safety regulations applied to different practical areas may cause some of the variation, but it is more often due to the fact that staff can be fiercely independent and will want to use their own approach to behaviour management. It is essential, however, that all staff approach the management of behaviour in a consistent manner. In achieving this, it may help to develop a Consistency Model.

Consistency model for dealing with challenging behaviour from groups of students

Developing their own Consistency Model will help teams of staff to reflect on their appropriate behaviour management.

Reflection on practice

1 Get staff to identify five types of poor behaviour presented by groups of students. The following list of typical challenging behaviours may help in this:

- Low level disturbances

- Attention seeking behaviour

- Late arrival at class

- Lack of equipment

- Out of seat – wandering around and disturbing others

- Bickering amongst students

- Lack of motivation/apathy

- Hiding students' equipment

- Throwing things

- Shouting out

- Swearing

- Refusing to work/defiance

- Disruptive/argumentative behaviour

- Intimidation of staff

- Violence/aggression

- Bullying

2 Choose five different colours of paper and allocate one to each of these behaviours.

3 Then divide staff into groups of five. Each group member is given one of the five different coloured pieces of paper.

4 Each member of staff is then responsible for recording the two agreed strategies to deal with the allocated problem behaviour.

5 After 15 minutes specialist colour groups are formed. Staff with the same colour piece of paper assemble together. They then come up with the five best strategies to deal with their specialist behaviour.

6 The five best strategies for each of the five behaviours can then be placed on one side of a sheet of A4 paper as a Consistency Model Chart. Staff will then be expected to apply any of these strategies, but only these strategies, when faced with the listed challenging behaviours.

To help in the development of the Consistency Model described above, the remainder of this chapter lists a range of different challenging behaviours that students display and offers strategies you may like to use in managing them.

Low level disturbance – tapping pen/banging chair or table/ fiddling with gadgets

- Move closer to noisy student. Ask about their work rather than disturbance

- State that item/equipment should be put away or it will be kept by you until end of lesson. Keep it friendly. Remove item if necessary

- Check reasons for disturbance in a calm voice. Acknowledge good reasons from the student, then state 'Perhaps it wasn't your fault [students name], but get on with the task and we'll get it sorted at the end.'

- Use non-verbal signals to reduce disturbance – fingers to lips

- Don't overreact and don't demand the impossible ('I want total silence for the last 50 minutes!')

- Refer to disturbance behaviour, but carry on with session. Don't let students' actions disturb your session

- Pause momentarily and look directly at student – say nothing

- Involve student in session

- Give support strategies to student to improve concentration/listening skills

Attention seeking behaviour

- Tactically ignore the behaviour

- Change location in room for main protagonist(s) – isolate them

- Give student a choice – 'Continue to behave in this manner and the likely consequence will be [x]'

- Use tactical pausing – name student, click your fingers, pause for 5 seconds, then give your instruction

- Use proximity – move into student's personal space bubble, just stand behind them and say nothing

- Give student take-up time to comply – use stopwatch to time the lag/delay time and detain student at end of session for time wasted

- Use 'broken record' technique to gain compliance – repeat command and block/ignore any comments student makes

- When attention seeking behaviour is being displayed pause mid-sentence and remain silent until compliance is achieved

- Accentuate the positives

Late arrival at class

Lateness can have a most damaging effect on the lesson. Students arriving late contrive to disturb and disrupt your lesson to the maximum. In many cases it is best to tactically ignore late arrivers. Any strategies you do use should have a minimum impact on your lesson.

- Set ground rules for punctual arrival during the establishment phase at the beginning of the year. Arrange protocols/strategies that you will use for late arrivers

- Get student to fill in a grid with reason for late arrival. Signal late arrivers to sit:

  - At an appropriate moment issue them with a piece of paper divided into six squares

  - Get them to fill in one square with the following information – date, subject, number of minutes late, reason and signature

  - On the sixth occasion photocopy the sheet, retaining one copy and handing the other to the Pastoral coordinator or the School Links coordinator

  - Arrange for them to send a copy of the sheet home. Most students say they don't care if parents are informed, but they do – 'doesn't care … really does care!'

- Minimize disruption to class. Quickly ask reason for lateness and make it clear you will deal with it later

- With groups of students 'showboating' by making a grand late entry, wrong foot them by not allowing them to disrupt lesson. Ask them to wait outside or get them to settle in seats quickly. Deal with group later

- One member of group may wait outside and then enter when you are tactically ill-prepared. Be prepared

- Have a Late Chair in class. By arriving late student loses freedom to sit in normal seat. Student sitting in the Late Chair has to recap session to rest of the group at the end

- Have a variety of seats reserved for latecomers scattered around room. Ensure these are in low profile areas and perhaps in locations where they would lose street credibility to sit there

- Ensure student makes up lost time at break

- Issue positive rewards to those students arriving on time

Lack of equipment

- Keep an emergency stock of spare equipment

- Trade your pen for a piece of their equipment – to ensure return

- Encourage college to sell equipment

- Take photo of student holding up pencil case/equipment at beginning of year. Bring out photo when equipment is forgotten to remind student of how they were

- At start of lessons students have 30 seconds to sort out lack of equipment otherwise given 1st strike and 30 seconds' detention

- If pen is forgotten give student a green ink biro. Easy then to keep track of number of times pen is forgotten when you look through their work. Also green ink doesn't give them street credibility

- 'Points make Prizes' – students lose points for forgetting equipment. Student with the most points in class at end of week/term wins a prize

- Rewards for having correct equipment – praise/points/prizes

- Include agreement on equipment in contract signed by student

Out of seat

- Make your expectations about seating clear at beginning of term

  ❑ No moving out of seat without permission

  ❑ Can move out of seat when changing activity – from whole class work to group work

  ❑ Opportunities for moving out of seat will be limited

- Warn of consequences and carry them out. The time a student is out of their seat without permission is the time that they will be detained

- Change position of 'wanderers' – make them sit in front of your desk

- Reward and praise students who stay seated

- Have structured opportunities that will allow students to move

- Include some activities that allow movement. The majority of IFP 14–16 year old students are Kinaesthetic Learners; use activities that will engage them

- Have 'packed lessons' with lots of activities

Talking

Chatter while lecturer is talking

- Establish a take-up time for groups to settle during the establishment phase at the beginning of the year. For example – 2 minutes. Give a countdown with 30 seconds to go. After countdown, if quiet is not achieved hold up a stopwatch to record the time they are wasting. This will then relate to detention time at the end of the session. Once threatened you must follow it through and keep them in. Remember the 'certainty not severity' rule from earlier. The beep of the stopwatch will soon trigger the settling down and quiet

- Have a start-up activity for students to do when they arrive

- Get students involved at the beginning. Feedback from things learnt in the last session or things they wish to learn this session. Get students to echo back your instructions

- Use activities that test their listening skills. For example – jumbled letters relating to subject key words

- Give instructions to the class in a quiet voice. The chatterers will soon be quiet if they cannot hear

- Circulate the room and stand next to students who are chatting

- Switch lights on and off to gain attention and quiet

- Get students who are chatting to stand up

- Praise, acknowledge and reward those who are complying

- In setting up class routines in the establishment phase agree a rule that only one person can speak at any one time. They put their hand up to speak or a token is passed around and a person can only speak when they have the token

Chatter at the end of the lesson

- Interesting activity at the end of the lesson as a reward, if quiet at appropriate times

- Issue of rewards at end of lesson – keep all guessing who will receive them

- Have a quiz at lesson end and those who answer question can leave first. This is a very effective way of getting quiet. Usually ask questions standing at the front in quiet voice. Students at the back will soon realize that the front ones are leaving first and will quieten down

Bickering among students

- Separate them

- Re-organize seating or change activity

- Stand nearby to those bickering – invade their personal space

- Stop class and ask students to share their comments

- Remove perpetrators from class and talk to them. Try to get to the bottom of the issue and resolve it if you can

- It may be necessary to refer the incident to pastoral staff – they may have a bigger picture. Support structure may be involved (counsellor or anti-bullying groups)

- Use cooperative learning strategies that involve all learners working together

- Parents may need to be contacted

Lack of motivation/apathy

- Variety of tasks

  - ❑ Challenging work

  - ❑ Fixed tasks to be completed within limited time (for example, by time music finishes)

  - ❑ Include practical activities/games/fun, perhaps with an element of competition

- Set short-term targets

  - ❑ Rewards available when tasks completed (instant gratification)

- Get students involved in setting tasks

- Variety in teaching/learning styles

- Give verbal praise in public and reprimand in private

- Immediate display of work

- Make relevance of work clear – avoid 'what is the point of this?' comments

- Pair students who lack motivation with higher ability students

- If it continues to be a problem, student must make up work in their own time or work in isolation/in a colleague's class

Hiding other students' equipment

- To reduce risk sit students away from belongings – only have things that they need on their desk

- Agree expectations of behaviour in respect of other people's possessions in the establishment phase

- Sit likely suspects away from other students

- To avoid lesson disruption, get rest of class working on a task before looking for student's missing equipment

- Sometimes students think items have been taken when in fact they have mislaid them. Ensure they check bags and lockers thoroughly

Throwing things

- Clearly issue a rule reminder about throwing

- Make sure Health and Safety issues are covered

- Ensure you give a measured response – not in the heat of the emotional moment

- Isolate the perpetrator or re-group students if a number are involved

- Try to circulate around the room regularly

- Ensure the room is tidy when students arrive (makes it easier to detect thrown objects)

- Face students at all times. Ensure you have a full field of vision. For example – make use of OHP/electronic whiteboard

- Do not allow students to crowd around you for help, thus obscuring your vision. Establish the rule that students are helped one at a time

- Give time out from the classroom for a student who throws something

Shouting out in class

- When students shout out remind them of the rules

- Praise those students who do not shout out

- If shouting out occurs, use stopwatch and detain for length of time your lesson was disturbed

- Use three 'strikes' system. After third strike sanction is applied

- Tactical ignoring of some shouting out may be beneficial. Ignore them until they conform

- Reinforce the no shouting rule by reminding students prior to asking a question

- Consider a 'no hands up' ethos – staff nominate students to answer

Swearing

- Explain that in a work-related setting where customers may be within earshot swearing cannot be tolerated

- Get students to explain the meaning of swear words they use. Show you are not phased/embarrassed

- Have a Swear Box

- Record them swearing and play it back to them

- Use the paper with six boxes on it (as with lateness) to record when and what was said and why it was said

Refusing to work/defiance

- Check with them the reason for refusal/non-cooperation. Do they understand the task?

- Avoid conflict – look at student and address them by name quietly, firmly and with respect. Focus on the behaviour. Remind them about rules and routines. Remind them of past successes. Offer the opportunity to retrieve the situation

- Explain that their behaviour is not appropriate in terms of the Code of Behaviour. Preface it by telling them you think they can work well and that they need to make a decision about their behaviour. Give them time to reflect and come back for their decision

- Use the following script in difficult situations – 'if you choose to continue to [x] then I will have to [x], but if you choose another route then no sanction will be applied. I will give you 2 minutes to think it over.'

- Consider lecturer proximity. Circulate room. Offer quiet but firm encouragement and praise

- Ensure verbal, non-verbal and written rewards are used

- Change tactics/approach. For example, move student to another seat in the room

- Write names on the board of students refusing to work (three strikes and out)

- In some cases it may be appropriate to ignore the behaviour and deal with it later

- Avoid demanding an apology and do not brood on an act of defiance

- Call for support if necessary

Disruptive/argumentative behaviour

- Establish ground rules at the beginning and revisit them throughout the year
- Stay calm – ensure you are calm and use confident and strong body language. Avoid confrontation
- Remove student from their audience and the 'oxygen of publicity' and discuss situation one to one
- Give reasons why such behaviour is not acceptable
- Allow some 'cool-off' time – give student a Time Out Card
- Turn lights on and off as an attention diverter when students are disruptive
- Give rewards when positive language and cooperative behaviour is displayed
- Role model positive behaviour you wish to see
- Reinforce good behaviour through praise
- Make connections with students
- Use humour to distract students when they are particularly argumentative
- Have agreed non-verbal cues to signal to a student when they are becoming disruptive
- Rearrange seating plan – it may be best to move a student
- Introduction of paired working may reduce disruption

Intimidation of staff by students – put-downs/criticism/ignoring you

- Remain calm, cool and collected. Ensure body language shows confidence
- Don't always give student the desired and expected response
- Don't be phased by criticism directed at you, reflect on it. Show preparedness to accept/maybe change
- Talk to other staff – is same attitude shown towards them? If not – why not?
- Try befriending student, who may then be less inclined to behave badly towards you
- Get support of colleague or senior manager if you feel situation is serious
- A 'cool-off' period may be required
- Give student a choice within the rules
- Exercise Zero Tolerance with clear exit strategy and follow-up:

❑ Red Card

❑ Mentoring – anger management strategies

❑ Involve parents

❑ Instigate consequences

❑ Agree method of reparation

■ When students are ignoring you:

❑ Try a humorous approach

❑ Take the route of minimum disruption – 'You are ignoring me now. I'll see you later'

❑ Plan an escape route – 'I have asked you twice. Are you going to do as I have asked or do we have to take it further?'

❑ Appeal to their sense of good manners

Violence

When faced with violence it is important that your safety and that of other students is protected. With that in mind these tips may be useful:

■ Be calm, look relaxed and keep movement to a minimum. Do not invade their space.

■ Do not stand between student and door

■ Say nothing, count to ten

■ Assess level of threat/violence

■ If safe to do so, move between aggressor and victim. If aggression is directed at you, stand sideways, keep still, speak quietly

■ Address student by name, speaking quietly. You may need to show partial agreement – 'I can see how you feel'

■ Avoid sarcasm. Try using distractions

■ Try to diffuse situation, allow face-saving and introduce a cooling-off period

■ Later, give student strategies for anger management and counselling

■ Ensure you know the institute policy on violence – how to summon help and policies on restraint

Bullying

Depending on seriousness of incident it may be necessary to:

- Ensure victim is safe – remove from situation

- Ensure victim has advocates/supporters

- Gather information about incident

- Apply a no-blame approach

- Remove bully from situation

- Contact 14–16 coordinator. Ensure school has information and where possible parents are informed

- Try to resolve situation by discussing incident with bully, victim and advocates

- Use peer mediators

Much good material on bullying can be found at Kidscape 'www.kidscape.org.uk'.

Reflection on practice

Identify two types of challenging behaviour from among those discussed in this chapter and for each list the strategies you have used and indicate whether they were successful. Then list a further two new strategies you will use for each behaviour next term, based on those included in the chapter.

Key points to remember

It is important to develop a consistent approach in your college to manage the variety of challenging behaviours you meet.

- Spend time developing with your team your own Consistency Model where you identify key behaviours and a variety of strategies all team members will employ

- Identify the types of student behaviour that cause you the most concern and identify strategies suggested in this chapter which you will use

Reflection on Practice: Strategies for facing challenging behaviour

Behaviour One: _____

| Your own strategies you have used when faced with this type of behaviour | Successful | Unsuccessful |

| New strategies you will try in the next term | Successful | Unsuccessful |

Behaviour Two: _____

| Your own strategies you have used when faced with this type of behaviour | Successful | Unsuccessful |

| New strategies you will try in the next term | Successful | Unsuccessful |

CHAPTER 10

Using the whole team: behaviour management strategies for support staff

This chapter looks at:

- a range of tips for support staff to use with 14–16 year old learners in:

  ❑ informal settings, e.g. reception, office or finance, site staff, catering staff

  ❑ formal settings, e.g. learning resources/library staff, learning support, counsellors etc.

- key behaviour management strategies

- five case studies

The forgotten group in some colleges in relation to Behaviour Management staff development are support staff. In college 14–16 year old learners come into daily contact with a range of support staff in the following areas:

- counselling and guidance

- learning resources and library staff

- learning support assistants

- mentoring

- office/reception

- refectory/catering

- security

- site staff, including caretakers and cleaners

- technical support – for example Design and Technology, ICT

It is important that these key workers, who have lots of face-to-face contact with learners in informal and formal settings, are given appropriate strategies and skills to use. This could be done as a key point of induction for support staff.

Informal settings

Some support staff come into contact with students in informal settings away from the classroom. Students in the 14–16 age group find it difficult to adapt to the freedom they experience in a college, the large number and age range of students, the vastness of most college sites and the lack of supervision in their free time. When they meet site, security and canteen workers in public areas they do not have the maturity to handle interaction with some staff well, they will play to an audience and display 'showboating' behaviour. In those situations it is best to move students away to a setting where they will not be in the spotlight – to the corner of the refectory or, if in a corridor, a short distance away from the audience – ensuring at all times that you do not make yourself vulnerable.

Some situations that might occur in a variety of informal settings are given below.

Reception/office/finance

- **Challenging parents/carers**: Parents and carers often come into public areas and cause problems with their challenging and extreme behaviour. It is important to move them to another location and, if possible, get them seated to let them get whatever it is off their chests and then to reply. Asking the miracle question 'What would you like me to do to remedy this situation?' can take the wind out of their sails.

  Staff teams develop specific roles to play when dealing with different situations:

  ❏ The Rottweiler: takes no prisoners and can be very firm

  ❏ The Carer: listens, provides tissues and a shoulder to cry on

  ❏ The Problem Solver: tries to find a solution whilst showing empathy

- **Challenging/upset students**: Students can express a range of concerns when they come: when things are not right on a course, when they have timetable problems, when getting exam results, or when they have problems with their EMA (Educational Maintenance Allowance). The strategies to use are similar to those with challenging parents. Listen to the problem, allow the student to unload feelings and then try to find a solution.

Site staff, including security team

Often students will deliberately challenge staff in uniform, such as security staff. As a way of life they have learnt to challenge authority figures. Many will have met security staff in shopping centres/nightclubs and will displace their resentment from these settings onto college security staff.

Security staff usually work in teams of three or four. It is important that team members understand their roles clearly. One team I have worked with ascribed certain roles to team members. One had a listening role, to let students describe their feelings on a situation, another one had a 'tough, no messing role', a very firm figure. Another team I worked with were very pro-active, seeing a real problem with 14–16 year old learners who had 2 hours of unsupervised time in the middle of the day because of timetabling problems. This led to lots of damage, graffiti on site and students wandering the corridors disturbing other groups, so they decided to set up 5-a-side football activity during this time in the sports hall. This intervention reduced the problem behaviour and was also a way of developing positive relationships between the security team and students.

Often the security team will have to deal with adults trying to gain entry to the site, they will encounter students who forget passes and on occasions students will need to be removed from the learning environment. The skills that security staff have in diffusing conflict and confrontation should be used to train other staff.

Site staff often have to deal with students damaging property, smoking on site, dropping litter and cigarette ends. Students are very good at challenging staff in these situations and taking their poor behaviour to the limit. They also test staff, attempting to get them to lose their temper. A form of entrapment can take place. It is important that staff are aware of this and develop strategies to keep calm and to remain in control. They should utilize strategies outlined in Chapter 7 on Managing Confrontation.

Refectory/catering staff

Students will use these areas at a variety of times throughout the day, making supervision extremely difficult. Students in the 14–16 age group find it difficult to manage unsupervised/free time and tend to gravitate to these areas, where they can cause problems. Also the additives and ingredients in some products can cause poor behaviour within a short time of consumption, which can exacerbate the situation. Some stealing of food and damage to vending machines can occur. Also students can be abusive to staff.

It is important that there is a clear policy for managing behaviour in these areas and that there is a clear support structure available – such as the ability to call security or other support staff. Aiding the identification of students through photo files may also be helpful.

Other learners

Given the wide age range of learners, some find it difficult to adapt to the perceived immature behaviour, particularly initially, of 14–16 year old learners. They can be noisy and disruptive and can disturb other students in learning resource areas and when moving along corridors past classrooms. It is important during induction to give 14–16 year old learners expectations of behaviour, particularly in unsupervised time. Also let older learners know about all the groups of learners they are likely to meet in college.

Some learners at 16+ are concerned about the attitude and advances made by some 14–16 year old learners. They can be genuinely frightened and do not know how to respond to protect themselves from their advances.

Formal settings

Learning resource/library staff

Library staff contribute directly to the learning process, teaching research skills to students and developing other skills in learners to ensure that they are able to study independently. One main challenge of working in library areas is that students from a variety of groups and ages will come to study normally without lecturer supervision. Most resources/library areas are zones where quiet working is expected. Some students find this a real challenge. In one library they have helped to overcome this by giving students key study/research skills which will enable them to study independently. They have also zoned the library into Red, Amber and Green zones. The red zone is a silence zone so learners can study and work without disturbances. The amber zone is one where quiet talking is allowed and the green zone is one where learners can move around freely, be active in their learning and discuss work openly with other learners. This system is working well.

With many libraries now reducing book stock and up to 90 per cent of materials being electronic this has introduced the need for a new range of skills for learners and support staff. The widespread use of the Internet has also caused another challenge, with students attempting to access inappropriate sites. It is possible to block most of these, but some students are able to circumvent these systems. Software is available to monitor live usage and some colleges have introduced staff team members who will monitor usage and move quickly to challenge students who may be on inappropriate sites – with evidence that could be sent to parents/carers.

Learning support workers/mentors/counsellors/guidance

The work of these staff could be compromised by them adopting an overly disciplinarian approach. Much of their work is based on trust. In fact, these workers need to have the following qualities:

- listener
- able to display positive non-verbal communication
- encourager
- aim to raise self-esteem
- act as a role model
- empathetic
- open and sharing their own life experiences
- supporting
- non-judgemental

So, when dealing with learners it is important that they use strategies that will not compromise their role.

Key behaviour management strategies for support staff

- When dealing with challenging behaviour do not conduct it in a public forum – remove student from the oxygen of publicity

- Keep your focus on the behaviour, do not personalize it

- Positioning is important:

  - ❏ move learner to a new position (much like a football referee when they are about to issue a yellow card to a player)

  - ❏ do not have your back to a number of learners – position yourself with the wall behind you

  - ❏ always have an escape route

  - ❏ stand at right angles to the learner as this will avoid excessive eye contact

- Do not invade student's personal space bubble (46 cm around most people). An angry student has a larger space bubble

- Do not get dragged into arguments. The student will try to display a range of secondary behaviours to divert your attention from the primary behaviour you are addressing. Examples include huffing, looking away, tut-tutting. Re-focus learner by repeating primary behaviour/misdemeanour you are addressing

- Focus on the required behaviour – say what student should be doing not what they shouldn't be doing

- Avoid over-verbalising

- Speak slowly, vary pace and lower pitch

- Use silence and pauses. Leaving 3–5 seconds after a statement with eye contact can be powerful

- Use open body language – have a relaxed position

- Stay positive

- Use attention diverters

- Allow student and yourself time out or time to reflect

- Keep your own and their respect intact

- Allow student to save face by giving them an escape route

- Use de-escalation skills

- Do not be manically vigilant – tactically ignore some things

Reflection on practice

Below are five real scenarios presented by support staff in which they have faced challenging behaviour.

Read each one and select which of the strategies given would be best to use. Then add another appropriate strategy of your own.

Scenario 1: Learning resource centre

A student is asked by the librarian to leave the library after several warnings. He has made rude noises, played music on his MP3 player and played games on the computer. He refuses to leave and then threatens to 'knock the librarian's block off'.

Strategy 1: Call for security team to remove student. This threat is serious and is likely to lead to a severe consequence for the learner, so you must ensure the incident is recorded and details passed on to your line manager.

Strategy 2: Call for colleague support and request that the student leaves.

Personal strategy:

Scenario 2: ICT suite

A support tutor is frequently being asked to help a student in a busy ICT session. The student's demands are unrealistic and she is wanting personal attention. She becomes frustrated and finally becomes very abusive with the support tutor, who is trying to support learners with Special Educational Needs.

Strategy 1: The support tutor would need to outline the problem to the lecturer working with the group and get their support and help with the student.

Strategy 2: Explain to the student that you are busy with another student but that you will help them when you have finished.

Strategy 3: Elicit the support of another student to help until further support becomes available.

Personal strategy:

Scenario 3: Site staff

Three students from the Creative and Media area are dumping bags of rubbish at the back of the block in front of fire doors when the caretaker asks them to remove it and place it in the correct area. They ignore him and walk off muttering.

Strategy 1: Follow the students back to their classroom, speak to the lecturer about what has just happened and get them to rectify the situation and apologise.

Strategy 2: Follow the students and speak to them about the Health and Safety issues of what they have done and the likely consequence of blocking fire doors.

Strategy 3: Ignore the incident and clear away the rubbish, as it will take less time.

Personal strategy:

Scenario 4: Refectory/catering

A group of students are rude to staff serving hot food at the servery; they say that the food portions are too small and that they are not going to pay for it and they swear at the staff.

Strategy 1: Tell the students that refusing to pay is their choice, and retain the food.

Strategy 2: Tell the students that there are consultative procedures that they can use (for example, the College Consultative Committee, or Student Union representatives). They should use these to air their views.

Strategy 3: Clearly remind students about college policy relating to swearing and remind them of the consequences if they continue. Use of a photo file may be needed to identify students.

Personal strategy:

Scenario 5: Learning support assistant

A learning support worker is attempting to help a student with Special Educational Needs who is refusing the help and support being offered. Other students in the room are teasing the student because he is receiving help.

Strategy 1: Discuss the actions of other students with the lecturer and explain how this is restricting the help you can give to the student with SEN. Get the lecturer to talk to the students concerned.

Strategy 2: Discuss with the student you are supporting the reasons for their refusal to accept help and offer alternative strategies.

Strategy 3: Discuss with the student whether working with them in an alternative location might be better.

Personal strategy:

Support staff have a range of skills in management of behaviour that they could share with and develop with lecturers. I believe that they are a powerful under-used resource and that colleges should utilize this resource fully by developing a team approach to managing behaviour. This will help to develop a consistent approach to behaviour management amongst *all* staff.

Key points to remember

■ Importance of induction programme for support staff that includes behaviour management strategies

■ Adopting a teamwork approach between lecturers and support staff in relation to behaviour management

■ Involve support staff in the development of Code of Conduct for learners

■ Understanding key strategies to use with learners in typical settings. Strategies will vary depending on role and whether in a formal or informal setting

CHAPTER 11

Staff development activities

The 20 activities contained in this chapter are regularly used on Staff Development/Training Days by the author. The same activities are also on the associated CD Rom. These are photocopiable resources which can be freely used within the purchaser's institution for staff development purposes.

- The instructions are written from the viewpoint of the facilitator

- Group sizes for activities vary:

  ❑ Activity 1 – a minimum of at least 15 delegates will be needed

  ❑ Activities 5, 14 and 15 – at least 9 delegates will be needed

  ❑ All other activities will work with numbers that can split into multiples of 2, 3 or 5

ACTIVITY 1: *OUR TOP TEN*

Area: To identify key types of poor behaviour

Resources: Flipchart paper per group

Group Size: 5

Duration: 20 minutes

- Get each group of 5 to decide their own Top Ten of Challenging Behaviours, with Number 1 being the most intrusive and challenging behaviour

- Get 3 groups of 5 to join together and refine their 3 lists into one Top Ten

- Get one member from each group of 15 to take their Top Ten and meet with leaders of other groups

- A super Top Ten can then be produced

- This list can be used as a basis of other activities during the day – for example, Consistency Model Activity

ACTIVITY 2: *AUDITS FOR STAFF*

Area: Development of audits for staff to use to make their learning environments conducive for good work and behaviour

Resources: Worksheet for task below per group. (Also refer to Reflection on Practice: Classroom Audit Sheets in Chapter 4)

Group Size: 3

Duration: 20 minutes

- Get delegates to 'thought shower' the key areas involved in ensuring that learning environments are conducive for good work and behaviour. Examples could include:

  ❏ Different learning styles

  ❏ Rules and routines

  ❏ Consistency in behaviour management

  ❏ Positive behaviour management

  ❏ Use of support staff

  ❏ Peripheral learning

  ❏ Differentiation

  ❏ Assessment for learning

  ❏ Relationships

  ❏ Furniture arrangement and seating plans

- From this list select 5 areas and get group members to make up 20 questions/statements for each area onto the task sheet

- *Questions 1–10* will require Yes or No responses. The questions must be phrased so that the Yes response is the one that would lead to a conducive environment for good work and behaviour

- *For Questions 11–20* list 10 statements and get staff to develop a 1–5 scoring system for each statement, with 5 being when there is strong agreement with the statement and 1 when there is strong disagreement with the statement. Again the statements outline a desired position to do with good work and behaviour

- Get them to join together with two other groups and compare their questions/statements

Classroom audit

Circle YES or NO to these statements:

1   YES/NO

2   YES/NO

3   YES/NO

4   YES/NO

5   YES/NO

6   YES/NO

7   YES/NO

8   YES/NO

9   YES/NO

10   YES/NO

TOTAL NUMBER OF 'YES' RESPONSES TO STATEMENTS 1–10   ......

Circle 1, 2, 3, 4 or 5 where 1 = STRONGLY DISAGREE and 5 = STRONGLY AGREE:

11   1 2 3 4 5

12   1 2 3 4 5

13   1 2 3 4 5

14   1 2 3 4 5

15   1 2 3 4 5

16   1 2 3 4 5

17   1 2 3 4 5

18   1 2 3 4 5

19   1 2 3 4 5

20   1 2 3 4 5

TOTAL SCORE FOR RESPONSES TO STATEMENTS 11–20   ......

ACTIVITY 3: *POSITIVE LEARNING ENVIRONMENT – 10 Rs*

Area: Developing a positive learning environment

Resources: Worksheet for task below per group

Group Size: 2

Duration: 20 minutes

The 10 Rs of Positive Behaviour Management listed in Chapter 4 were:

- Rules

- Routines

- Recognition

- Rapport

- Respect

- Relationships

- Rights

- Responsibility

- Resilience

- Rewards

- In groups of 2, get staff to list how they would utilize these 10 areas in their learning environments. For example, how would they establish rules and routines initially and maintain them throughout the year. Ask them to jot down any ways that they use these areas on the sheet provided.

The 10 Rs of Positive Behaviour Management

Rules	
Routines	
Recognition	
Rapport	
Respect	
Relationships	
Rights	
Responsibility	
Resilience	
Rewards	

ACTIVITY 4: *ENDORPHIN RELEASE*

Area: Developing a positive approach to managing behaviour

Resources: Worksheet for the task below per group

Group Size: 2

Duration: 10 minutes

- Point out to the staff that when thinking about how to develop a positive learning environment it may be best to consider the things that affect them in schools/colleges

- Ask the staff to make a list of what turns *them* from a relaxed to a stressful state throughout the day

- Then ask them to list things that would make *them* feel better through the day

- When they have completed the task, point out that it is important they try to replicate for *students* many of the things that make them feel better if they are to develop a positive atmosphere in the classroom

DEVELOPING A POSITIVE ATMOSPHERE

Stress factors:

1.

2.

3.

4.

5.

Things that could have made you feel better:

1.

2.

3.

4.

5.

ACTIVITY 5: *SEE AND HEAR*

Area: Reflecting on learning environments where there is good or bad behaviour

Resources: Flipchart paper per group

Group Size: 3

Duration: 20 minutes

- Ask the staff to divide into groups of 3

- Ask each group to consider for 5 minutes what they might see and hear in a learning environment where there is poor behaviour

- Then get the group to consider for 5 minutes what they might see and hear in a learning environment where there is good behaviour

- Get each group to join with 2 other groups to agree a list of key factors of positive learning environments

ACTIVITY 6: *BLOCKING AND 'BROKEN RECORD' TECHNIQUE*

Area: Assertiveness and conflict management

Resources: Paper for all participants

Group Size: 3

Duration: 15 minutes

To manage some forms of poor behaviour and counter arguments from students it may be necessary to block their responses and to utilize the 'broken record' technique. Use of these techniques can also be useful when we are being assertive.

'Blocking' involves ignoring the comment made by a student and repeating our re-directing statement – rather like the repetition of the same line in a song when a crack in a record causes the needle to stick and repeat the same line.

- Ask staff to divide into groups of 3 with one person being the student, another the member of staff and the third person being an observer

- Ask each group to re-enact one of these situations which may cause a dispute:

  ❑ A student arriving 10 minutes late to your lesson for the third time this week

  ❑ A student failing to hand in a piece of coursework following a third extension

- Get the groups to swap roles and do the same thing

- Get all staff back together to analyse the best scripts to use when using the blocking and broken record technique

ACTIVITY 7: *ROLE PLAY*

Area: Developing positive body language

Resources: Worksheet for the task below per group

Group Size: 3

Duration: 20 minutes

- Get staff to divide into groups of 3

- Get each group member to chose a role – student, lecturer or observer

- Ask them to establish a scenario they would like to enact. It should be one where there is a disagreement between the lecturer and the student

- For 5 minutes get them to carry out the role play – with the observer recording on the sheet the body language of the lecturer and student in two different ways: body language that helped to resolve the disagreement and body language that was less than helpful

- Then ask them to swap roles

- Finally, ask them what are their conclusions from the activity in relation to the importance of body language?

Developing positive body language

Scenario:

	Helpful body language	Unhelpful body language
Student		
Lecturer		

ACTIVITY 8: *TRUE LIES!*

Area: Developing positive body language

Resources: Worksheet for the task below for each participant

Group Size: 3

Duration: 15 minutes

■ Get the staff to form groups of 3. Ask them to take turns to list four facts about themselves – three true and one lie

■ The other two in the group record on their sheets the body language of the member who is completing the task

■ As a group they should try to identify which of each of the facts were lies

■ They should list the body language that indicated to them it was a lie

■ They should assess how successful they were as a group by starting with a maximum of 12 marks, and for each person's incorrect guess deduct 1 point up to a maximum of 4

True Lies!

Four facts about yourself:

1.

2.

3.

4.

Second person in group:

Body language

1.

2.

3.

4.

Third person in group:

Body language

1.

2.

3.

4.

Your Group's Score _____

ACTIVITY 9: *THE 4 Fs OF CONFRONTATION*

Area: Confrontation

Resources: Flipchart paper – 5 sheets per group

Group Size: 5

Duration: 20 minutes

When faced with confrontation students are often taken over by the emotion they are experiencing. All rational thought becomes impossible. We have a strong emotional arousal and we may respond in a less than appropriate manner. One of four F responses may occur:

- ■ Fight
- ■ Flight
- ■ Freeze
- ■ Flock

- ■ Ask staff to get into groups of 5 and use a sheet of flipchart paper for each of these F responses and list the types of situations which may cause students to respond in this manner

- ■ In the end they will have four sheets with a list of situations where students will respond with an F response

- ■ Ask the groups to list on the fifth sheet some strategies that they could use when faced with these types of responses

ACTIVITY 10: *COMMUNICATION BLOCKERS*

Area: Conflict management

Resources: Worksheet for the task below per group

Group Size: 2

Duration: 15 minutes

Some situations can turn into conflict when one person in a conversation deliberately uses communication blockers. Bad conversation habits can cause a communication breakdown.

- Divide groups into pairs with one person being A and the other B

- Person A initiates a conversation about a hobby or holiday location. Person B should practise the communication blockers listed on the task worksheet

- After 5 minutes A and B should swap roles

- Then ask them to discuss the following:

  ❑ How the speaker felt in each case.

  ❑ Could communication blockers lead to conflict?

  ❑ How could this exercise be used with students?

Examples of conversation blockers:

- Interrupting by talking loudly

- Challenging

- Contradicting

- Advising

- Dominating

- Accusing

- Probing

- Making judgements on what is said

- Interrupting

- Giving their opinion

- Trying to outdo the other speaker by having done something better

ACTIVITY 11: *ACTIVE LISTENING*

Area: Conflict management, positive behaviour management

Resources: Flipchart paper per group

Group Size: 3

Duration: 15 minutes

For effective communication the listener should always try to engage with the speaker by listening actively.

- Divide staff into groups of 3 and get them to make a list of five key characteristics of an active listener. The ones they should identify are:

  - They face the speaker and look into their eyes

  - They are relaxed, don't interrupt or fidget

  - They should summarize key points made by the speaker

  - If they do not understand something, at a suitable break they should ask for clarification

  - They nod agreement

- Once these characteristics have been identified, two members of the group should then start a conversation on music or food and utilize their active listening skills. The third member of the group should observe

- The observer should then feed back their views

- The two involved in the conversation should think about the following:

  - What was the easiest and most difficult thing about being an active listener?

  - Why is it important to be a good listener?

ACTIVITY 12: *LANGUAGE OF CHOICE*

Area: Scripts we use with students

Resources: Paper for each group

Group Size: 2

Duration: 10 minutes

The choice of words we use and how we say them are key to the successful management of behaviour. It is always good to prepare scripts for different situations. Remember the less we say the better. Also assume a pleasant tone – calm words are likely to result in calm students. Avoid overly apologetic or pleading language.

Some scripts we can use are as follows:

- 'If you choose to break our rules then you must understand the consequences you are bringing on yourself.'

- 'What is the rule for answering questions? Then please use it. Thank you.'

Some students will try to divert your attention by some secondary behaviour, perhaps by using counter-argument, 'You're always picking on me'. It is important that we keep our focus and block their response and repeat our instruction.

We can also give students a choice and some 'cool off' time to reflect on the situation: 'You realize that if you keep chewing gum the consequence you will bring on yourself – you will lose your breaktime. However, if you put the gum in the bin you will keep your break. I will give you a few minutes to think about it.'

- Discuss the points made above and then split staff into groups of 2

- Ask each group to think of a situation where they might be able to use Language of Choice.

- With one person acting as the student and the other as a lecturer practise the use of the script.

- Then reverse roles.

ACTIVITY 13: *HOW YOUR COLLEGE HELPS STUDENTS TO DEVELOP THEIR OWN STRATEGIES TO MANAGE THEIR BEHAVIOUR*

Area: Scripts we use with students

Resources: Worksheet for task below per group

Group Size: 5

Duration: 15 minutes

Many young learners find it extremely difficult to manage their emotions and feelings. We often tell students not to behave in a particular way without giving them the skills and strategies necessary to avoid that behaviour and to manage their feelings and emotions.

- Split staff into groups of 5 and ask each group to reflect on what they do as a college with students in the areas on the worksheet and what could be done to develop these areas in the future

How we are helping students develop their own strategies

	What we are currently doing	What we could do in the future
Raising learner self-esteem		
Using dramatherapy/role play with learners to manage anger		
Getting students to understand the influence of body language and position		
Developing active listening skills and reducing communication blockers		
Developing a script of positive statements/affirmations for students when facing a difficult situation		
Developing an alternative view/ mindset – for example someone bumping into you may not have done it intentionally		
Using/developing relaxation strategies with students – for example, breathing, counting and visualization		
Using mediators		
Understanding cycles of anger: – Signs/triggers – Actions to avoid		
Use of mirroring behaviour and modelling approaches to help students reflect on their own responses		

ACTIVITY 14: *WHEELS WITHIN WHEELS*

Area: Dealing with badly behaving groups

Resources: Paper for recorders in each group

Group Size: Groups of 9 subdivided into 3s

Duration: 25 minutes

- Choose 3 behavioural issues relating to badly behaving groups for each group of 9. There should be different issues for each group of 9

- Each group of 3 deals with one issue. It could be that they discuss strategies to deal with types of poor behaviour experienced by delegates in schools/colleges. Each group of 3 spends 5 minutes on their behaviour. One group member records findings and they then move to the next group (clockwise direction) taking their behaviour with them. This group spends 5 minutes adding strategies to the list. All group recorders move at the same time to new groups taking their behaviour with them. There will be 3 moves in all, with the group recorder returning to their original group where they share the strategies from the other 2 groups

- Each group then feed back strategies to all the other staff delegates

ACTIVITY 15: *HOT SEATING*

Area: Dealing with badly behaving groups

Resources: Flipchart and paper for 'hot seaters' in each group

Group Size: Groups of 9 subdivided into 3s

Duration: 20 minutes

- Subdivide staff into groups of 9

- Agree a list of challenging behaviours displayed by badly behaving groups of students and allocate different behaviours to each group of 9

- Each group of 9 subdivides into groups of 3 with each subgroup electing a leader to hot seat

- They have a sheet of paper on which they write the behaviour

- Each group then has 2 minutes to 'thought shower' strategies to use to manage this behaviour

- On 2 minutes whistle/wind chimes sound, all 'hot seaters' move to a new group

- Agree prior to this how hot seaters will move (e.g. clockwise)

- Hot seaters take their issue to new group where they have 3 minutes for tasks

- They read out strategies already listed then they 'thought shower' from group additional strategies for that behaviour

- This continues until the hot seater returns to their original group

- Findings are then collated and issued to staff delegates

ACTIVITY 16: *IDENTIFYING KEY STUDENT ROLES IN BADLY BEHAVING GROUPS*

Area: Dealing with badly behaving groups

Resources: Sheet with list of student roles per group

Group Size: 5

Duration: 10 minutes

Students play different roles in each class. The key to successful behaviour management is to identify their roles and use this to your advantage. Gaining the upper hand with the alpha males and alpha females in the group is the key to successful behaviour management.

■ Split staff into groups of 5 and each group should identify a class of students who offer high levels of challenging behaviour

■ Using the list, they should try to ascribe roles that key members of the class play and identify some strategies that may work to help to develop a good working atmosphere

■ Discuss what whole class reward systems could be developed to promote good relationships

Some key roles of students

- **Alpha male:** Above-average intelligence, usually physically bigger

- **Alpha female:** Above-average intelligence, dressed in the latest fashions, uses sarcasm to control

- **Instigator:** Starts trouble but usually gets away with it by being surreptitious

- **Regulator/Questioner:** Constantly interrupts asking the same question in many different ways

- **Deflector:** Takes the heat off a student in trouble by deflecting your attention by smart comments or minor misbehaviour

- **Orchestrator:** The student who co-ordinates much of the bad behaviour acting as a 'conductor' to the symphony of bad behaviour

- **Class Clown:** The class entertainer, who can be difficult to manage

- **Fall Guy:** Male or female student who is happy to take the rap for things

- **Challenger:** Enjoys challenging the rules and instructions given to them. They often 'grandstand' by making a late entrance – to gain the plaudits of their peer group

ACTIVITY 17: *PICTURE THIS*

Area: Assertiveness

Resources: Felt pens and flipchart paper per group

Group Size: 5

Duration: 15 minutes

- Divide staff into groups of 5

- Each group has a sheet of flipchart paper and felt pens

- Get each group to imagine what an assertive person may look like

- Then get the group to produce a drawing of an assertive person and label it to show their key attributes

- Get each group to display their drawings

- Facilitator then produces their own identikit of the key points raised by each group

ACTIVITY 18: *ASSERTIVENESSS 'THOUGHT SHOWER'*

Area: Assertiveness

Resources: Flipchart paper per group

Group Size: 5

Duration: 20 minutes

- ■ Divide staff into groups of 5

- ■ Get each group to 'thought shower' all the words that come into their heads to do with assertiveness onto the flipchart paper for 5 minutes

- ■ Get each group then to subdivide the list into positive and negative words by placing a plus sign next to positive words and a minus sign next to negative words

- ■ Each group member then discusses any words that link with their approach when they are being assertive

- ■ Finally get each group to produce their own definition of assertiveness

- ■ These, together with lists of words, should be displayed

- ■ The facilitator might then like to display their own definition of assertiveness

ACTIVITY 19: *BEING ASSERTIVE WITH STUDENTS*

Area: Assertiveness

Resources: List of assertiveness strategies per group

Group Size: 3

Duration: 15 minutes

- ■ Divide staff into groups of 3. One group member to take the role of lecturer, another a student and the third an observer

- ■ Select a scenario where a lecturer is having to reprimand the student. The student should be argumentative

- ■ The lecturer should practise assertiveness techniques in dealing with the obstructive and argumentative student. Some strategies/approaches that could be used are listed below

- ■ Get the observer to feed back their comments:

  - ❑ How successful was the assertive approach?

  - ❑ Are there any other assertiveness techniques that could have been used?

- ■ Change roles and repeat

Assertiveness strategies/approaches

- Decide what you want

- Ask for it clearly

- Be calm and relaxed

- Give and take criticism

- Have a confident tone in your speech and fluctuate levels. Use silence

- State how you would like behaviour to improve

- Think carefully about your non-verbal behaviour – for example, avoid nervous movements

- Try to end the conversation positively

ACTIVITIES 20: *WHAT DO YOU DO NEXT?*

Area: Case studies for lecturers

Resources: Case studies A–M below

Group Size: 3

Duration: 15 minutes

- Ask staff to divide into groups of 3

- Give each group a scenario to deal with (from Case studies A–M). Get the group to list the strategies they would use

- Get 2 groups of 3 to join together to describe their strategies and encourage each group to offer further strategies to the other

Case Studies

Case Study A

In a lesson a student repeatedly displays low level challenges. They are attention seeking, disruptive and are frequently off-task.

Case Study B

A group of students in class are uncooperative and are working together to provide a destructive influence.

Case Study C

A student arrives 5 minutes late at a lesson for a second time in a week. The student doesn't have a reason for lateness and has a 'so what' attitude.

Case Study D

A student arrives late after lesson has started. She enters the room, still wearing her coat. The student is asked to take off the coat. Once she complies she says a pen has leaked and she needs to put the pen in a bin. The lecturer tells her to wait. The student then blots her finger all over her book, sucks the ink and says she feels sick. She then says 'You had better let me out, as I am not clearing it up.'

Finally the student is allowed to sit outside in the fresh air. When she comes back in the room she disrupts the group. 'I've no pen now, you'll have to lend me one.' She then hides her head in her coat. Very little work is completed.

At the end of the lesson she demands to leave early as she has a train to catch. When her request is refused, she states, 'Then you'll have to take me home.' She was allowed to leave, with the rest of the class, when the bell rang.

Case Study E

A male student enters the room and refuses to remove his baseball cap or fleece. He finally takes his hat off after four requests. He has no book or pen, so the lecturer gives him a pen and some paper. He sits and does nothing. Despite requests he still refuses to work.

Whilst the rest of the class are working, he tries to distract other students. When asked to turn around and get on with his work, he accuses the lecturer of picking on him. He continues to turn around. The only thing done is that his paper is covered with doodles. When asked to work, he shouts out, accusing the lecturer of picking on him, which causes a major disruption.

The lecturer then asks him to leave the room. After a cooling off period, the lecturer sees him and tells him that he can return to the room if he agrees to work and stop disturbing others. He is uncooperative and denies that he has done anything wrong. He argues that others get away with not working. He becomes aggressive. The lecturer tells him to go to the Head of Department (HoD), the next stage in the Code of Behaviour. He refuses to go, so the HoD is called to the class. The student is removed.

Case Study F

A male student comes into the classroom wearing headphones belonging to his MP3 player. The music is playing loudly and he cannot hear anything you say. You ask him to remove the headphones and he fails to hear you. He looks down refusing to give you eye contact.

Case Study G

A student is using her mobile phone discretely under the desk to send a text message to another student in the room. The student on receiving the message becomes extremely distressed.

Case Study H

A 16 year old student enters the room in a loud manner after you have started the lesson. She sits down and starts swearing at other students. She then nudges and annoys students sitting next to her. Later she makes the worksheets into paper aeroplanes and throws them across the room.

Case Study I

A group of four 14 year old girls are mixing with a group of 19 year old boys on the perimeter of your site. They are smoking something and your suspicions are roused by the smell from the tobacco. Inappropriate comments are being made by the boys to the girls. When you speak to them about this both the girls and the boys become defensive and confrontational.

Case Study J

A group of 14 year old students are attempting to leave the site at lunchtime. You ask them to return to the site because of the Duty of Care role with younger learners. They argue with you, saying that they can leave the site at lunchtime. They become very abusive and start shouting out rude comments to you.

Case Study K

A student returns after a couple of days absence with a cough. He uses this to disrupt the start of the lesson. The lecturer suggests that he leave the room to get a drink of water. Several others then start coughing. Coughing is exaggerated and timed to coincide with every attempt of the lecturer to start the lesson. When asked to stop they say the problem is medical and they can't help it.

Case Study L

Five or six male 16 year old students persistently disrupt the class. They question everything the lecturer asks them to do and argue that they are being picked on. They make fun of the lecturer whilst she is trying to explain the work – they openly laugh at her. They throw things across the room, break any equipment that is loaned to them. They refuse to do the work saying they do not understand what to do and do not see the point of doing it. They accuse the lecturer of teaching irrelevant topics [which is not the case]. They draw on the tables and make rude comments to girls who are sitting on the tables in front of them. The girls have refused to sit where the lecturer asks them to. They arrive late and walk out of the room before the end of the lesson. When action is taken by the lecturer (for example, no equipment loaned, work written on board with no instruction for students to copy down) they accuse her of not teaching them properly and say they will complain.

Case Study M

A 15 year old on the Increased Flexibility Programme arrives in your lesson for the first time. He has missed your first two sessions. When he arrives he begins showboating and tries to disrupt the session. He interferes with other students and is shouting out comments. He is wearing a hat, outside coat and headphones. You ask him to settle quietly and remove his headphones, he refuses saying, 'You're not my real lecturer.' When you challenge him again he becomes very aggressive.

GLOSSARY OF KEY TERMS AND ACRONYMS IN SCHOOLS AND FURTHER EDUCATION

The most commonly used terms and acronyms are listed here. You can visit the following websites for a full set of definitions:

- www.qca.org.uk/14-19/toolkit/glossary.htm

- www.qaa.org.uk/aboutus/acronyms.asp

- www.lsc.gov.uk/hampshire-iow/corporate/jargonbusterinfo.htm

ALI:	Adult Learning Inspectorate.
Appraisal:	A system providing professional development for lecturers/teachers.
Attainment:	Where achievement is measured by the individual's knowledge, skills and understanding in a particular subject area.
Attainment Level (AL):	There are eight levels for each Attainment Target and the Attainment Level is the level at which a student is working.
Attainment Target (AT):	National Curriculum Assessments (SATs) test a number of these for each subject. A target sets out the knowledge, skills and understanding that students are expected to reach.
Banding:	Grouping students based on ability.
Benchmarking:	Comparison of two or more schools determining relative levels of success in examinations.
Capitation:	Money allocated for each teaching subject in school, controlled usually by head of department or subject coordinator.
Cognitive Ability Test (CAT):	A standardized test in non-verbal reasoning and mathematical skills, usually given in Year 7, with scores indicating the potential of a student.
Core subject:	One of three compulsory subjects (English, Maths and Science) within the National Curriculum.
CLAIT:	Computer Literacy and Information Technology.
Continuing Professional Development (CPD):	A variety of short- and long-term training programmes, some with option of accreditation, aiding employment-related knowledge and skills.
COVE:	Centre of Vocational Excellence.
Disapplication:	A small number of students may be disapplied from some of the National Curriculum because of Special Educational Needs.
E2E:	Entry to Employment.

EBP:	Education Business Partnership.
Education Welfare Officer (EWO):	LEA employed person who checks on attendance of learners and can provide welfare support.
EFL:	English as a Foreign Language.
EMA:	Education Maintenance Allowance.
Emotional and Behavioural Difficulty/Disorder (EBD):	Barriers to learning resulting from difficulties due to emotions or behaviours.
ESOL:	English to Speakers of Other Languages.
Further Education (FE):	Education for post-16 year olds, which is non-compulsory and not Higher Education.
Foundation Degree:	Two-year Higher Education qualification designed to meet skills shortages in certain fields. They are one level below an honours degree.
General Certificate of Secondary Education : (GCSE)	Examination taken by most students at the end of compulsory education (Year 11: 15–16 year olds). Examinations split into different tiers allowing students to access different grade bands.
General Teaching Council (GTC):	Regulatory body for teachers. Membership is compulsory for all teachers in England (www.gtce.org.uk).
Higher Education (HE):	Usually University level, including undergraduate, postgraduate and doctorate level.
In-class support:	Support provided by teaching assistants (TAs) in schools for individual students.
Individual Behaviour Plan (IBP):	A behavioural plan developed by the school in consultation with an individual student and parents to set out targets for the student and the support the school will provide to help the student to attain these goals.
IFP:	Increased Flexibility Programme.
INSET:	In-service education and training for teachers.
Individual Education Plan (IEP):	Programmes drawn up by school to provide support for students with learning difficulties and those who have exceptional ability.
Individual Learning Plan (ILP):	Plan completed by students towards the end of Key Stage 3 (age 14) listing progress and achievements and mapping out education and training across the 14–19 range
Key Stage (KS):	Students' progression through school is measured in Key Stages. KS1: 3–7 year olds. KS2: 7–11 year olds. KS3: 11–14 year olds. KS4: 14–16 year olds.
LEA:	Local Education Authority.
Learn Direct:	Free service offering information on adult education and courses.
Literacy:	A term referring to the necessary reading, writing and speaking skills a person needs to converse in society.
LLDD:	Learners with Learning Difficulties and Disabilities.
LSC:	Learning and Skills Council.

LSN:	Learning Skills Network.
MA:	Modern Apprenticeship.
MFL:	Modern Foreign Language.
Mid YIS:	Middle Years Information System
MLD:	Mild Learning Difficulties.
NQF:	National Qualifications Framework.
Number On/Off Roll (NOR):	Number of students enrolled at school.
Numeracy:	A term relating to general mathematical skills enabling person to perform simple tasks in society.
NVQ:	National Vocational Qualification.
Pastoral:	Refers to the social welfare of students at school. Schools are required to produce pastoral care policies to outline steps taken to ensure students' welfare.
Pastoral Support Plan:	School-based plan to help children manage their behaviour.
Peer Mentoring:	Where a student acts as a mentor to another student.
P levels/scales:	Performance levels designed for students with Special Educational Needs, for students who do not meet National Curriculum Level 1.
Post-Ofsted Action Plan:	A public document sent to all carers/parents of students at the school written by the governing body within 40 days of an Ofsted inspection highlighting key issues from the inspection.
Progress File:	A set of materials replacing the Record of Achievement designed to help students plan and review progress.
Pupil Referral Unit (PRU):	A school maintained by an LEA providing education to students excluded from schools.
QCA:	Qualifications and Curriculum Authority.
Record of Achievement (RoA):	A set of materials recording and reviewing pupil progress. Now replaced by the Progress File.
Standard Assessment Tests (SATs):	Tests in English, Maths and Science taken at 7, 11 and 14 years of age.
Special Educational Needs (SEN):	A student identified as having a learning disability resulting in underachievement.
SSCs:	Sector Skills Councils.
Teacher Training Agency:	The body that funds teacher education and accredits initial teacher training.
Value added:	Additional educational gain for a student from the school they attend.
VQ:	Vocational Qualification.
WBL:	Work-based Learning.
WP:	Widening Participation.
YP:	Young People.

REFERENCES AND FURTHER READING

Ballinger, E. (1996) *The Learning Gym*. Glasgow: Brainwise

Berry, I. (2003) *ALITE Newsletter*. November 2003. Available at www.alite.co.uk/newsletters/2003/november.htm (accessed 12 October 2006)

Besag, V. (2006) *Understanding Girls' Friendships, Fights and Feuds: A Practical Approach to Girls' Bullying*. Maidenhead: Open University Press

Blakemore, S. and Frith, U. (2005) *The Learning Brain: Lessons for Education*. Oxford: Blackwell

Blum, P. (2001) *A Teacher's Guide to Anger Management*. London: RoutledgeFalmer

Chandler, J. (2006) *Oppositional Defiant Disorder (ODD) and Conduct Disorder (CD) in Children and Adolescents: Diagnosis and Treatment*. Available at www.klis.com/chandler/pamphlet/oddcd/oddcdpamphlet.htm (accessed 13 April 2006)

Collett, P. (2004) *The Book of Tells*. London: Bantam Publishers

DfES (2003) *14–19: Opportunity and Excellence*. Nottinghamshire: DfES Publications

DfES (2005) *14–19 Education and Skills – White Paper*. Available at www.dfes.gov.uk/publications/14–19educationandskills (accessed 23 February 2005)

Diprose, J. and Burge, N. (2003) *Syndromes and Disorders*. Care Consultancy: South Devon

Fisher, M. (2005) *Beating Anger*. London: Random House/Rider

Food Standards Agency (2006) *Drinking Enough?* Available at www.eatwell.gov.uk/healthydiet/nutritionessentials/drinks/drinkingenough (accessed 14 December 2006)

Frieman, B. (2001) *What Teachers Need to Know About Children at Risk*. New York: McGraw-Hill

Gardner, H. and Hatch, T. (1989). Multiple intelligences go to school: educational implications of the theory of multiple intelligences. *Educational Researcher*, 18 (8), 4–9

George, B. (1995) *Gifted Education: Identification and Process*. London: David Fulton

Hall, E.T. (1959) *Silent Language*. New York: Doubleday and Co.

Jackson, C. (2006) *'Lads' and 'Ladettes' in School: Gender and a Fear of Failure*. Maidenhead: Open University Press

Jensen, E. (2003) *Environments for Learning*. San Diego, CA: The Brain Store

Jensen, E. (2005) Highly effective strategies for managing AD/HD. *Brain Store Teaching Tip of the Month* (Newsletter – April 2005). Available at www.thebrainstore.com (accessed 7 May 2005)

Kidscape (2006) Available at www.kidscape.org.uk (accessed 20 September 2006)

Kuhne, M., Schachar, R. and Tannock, R. (1997) Impact of comorbid oppositional or conduct problems on Attention-Deficit Hyperactivity Disorder. *Journal of the American Academy of Child and Adolescent Psychiatry*, 36 (12), 1715–1725

Lee, J. (1993) *Facing the Fire*. New York: Bantam

Long, R. and Fogell, J. (1999) *Supporting Pupils with Emotional Difficulties: Creating a Caring Environment for All*. London: David Fulton

Mathieson, K. and Price, M. (2002) *Better Behaviour in Classrooms: A Framework for Inclusive Behaviour Management*. London: Routledge/Falmer

Marland, M. (2001) *NAPCE Journal*, 19: 4 ((National Association of Pastoral Care in Education, University of Warwick)

Mehrabian, A. (1981) *Silent Messages: Implicit Communication of Emotions and Attitudes*. Belmont, CA: Wadsworth

Merrett, F. and Wheldall, K. (1990) *Positive Teaching in the Primary School*. London: Paul Chapman

Middle Years Information Systems (Mid YIS) (2006) Available at www.cemcentre.org/Render Page.asp?LinkID=11410000 (accessed 24 August 2006)

Moore, D. (2006) Education and Skills Committee – Minutes of Evidence. Oral Responses to Questions 1–47. Available at www.publications.parliament.uk (accessed 10 May 2006)

Northern, S. (2004) A rotten way to feed the children. *Times Educational Supplement*, 16 April 2004

O'Regan, F. (2002) *How to Teach and Manage Children with ADHD*. Wisbech: LDA

Osler, A., Street, C., Lall, M. and Vincent, K. (2002) *Not a Problem? Girls and School Exclusion*. London: National Children's Bureau

Pease, A. (2000) *Body Language: How to Read Others' Thoughts by their Gestures*. London: Sheldon Press

Pease, A. and Pease, B. (2002) *Why Men Lie and Women Cry*. London: Orion

Prashnig, B. (2006) *Learning Styles in Action*. London: Network Educational Press

Ribbens, G. and Thompson, R. (2001) *Understanding Body Language* (Barron's Business Success). Barron's Educational Series

Ribbens, G. and Thompson, R. (2002) *Body Language in a Week*. Abingdon: Hodder and Stoughton

Roffey, S. (2004) *The New Teacher's Survival Guide to Behaviour*. London: Paul Chapman

Rogers, B. (2004) *Cracking the Challenging Class*. Notes to DVD. Hendon: BooksEducation

Schmidt, T. (1993) *Anger Management and Violence Prevention. A Group Activities Manual for Middle and High School Students*. Johnson Institute

Vizard, D. (2003) *Behaviour Solutions for NQTs*. Available at www.behavioursolutions.com.

Vizard, D. (2004a) *Fuel for Thought*. Available at www.behavioursolutions.com

Vizard, D. (2004b) *Teaching 14–16 Year Olds in Colleges of Further Education*. Available at www.behavioursolutions.com.

Vizard (2006) *Syndromes and Conditions*. Available at www.behavioursolutions.com

Voakes, B. and King, C. (2004) *Jigsaw World Atlas*. London: Usborne Publishing

Wallis, C. (2004) What makes teens tick? *Time Magazine*, 7 June 2004, pp. 54–61

Watkins, C. (1999) *Managing Classroom Behaviour: From Research to Diagnosis*. London: Institute of Education, University of London

Wragg, T. (2002) *Times Education Supplement* ('Ask Ted')

Wyatt, P. (2002) The rise of the alpha girls, *Mail on Sunday*, 24 March 2002

Autism related site

www.autism.org

www.nas.org

Jargon/acronym busting websites

www.qca.org.uk/14-19/toolkit/glossary.htm

www.qaa.org.uk/aboutus/acronyms.asp

Starter activities/ideas

http://atschool.eduweb.co.uk/ufa10/starters/ – Starter activities

www.quizardry.com – Quiz/Starter ideas

Brain break ideas

www.braingym.org

Other useful websites

www.behavioursolutions.com – Articles and free newsletter on behaviour management issues

www.creativeclassrooms.com – Prashnig's Learning Style Profile website

www.gtce.org.uk – General Teaching Council

www.incentiveplus.co.uk – resources to promote emotional and behavioural skills

www.jlcbrain.com – Eric Jensen's Brain Learning website

www.kidscape.org.uk – useful site on bullying

INDEX